GREEN GUIDES

Crops in Pots

This is a **FLAME TREE** book
First published in 2011

Publisher and Creative Director: Nick Wells
Project Editor: Catherine Taylor
Art Director: Mike Spender
Layout Design: Dave Jones
Digital Design and Production: Chris Herbert
Picture Research: Laura Bulbeck, Polly Prior, Catherine Taylor
Proofreader: Tony Phillips
Indexer: William Jack

Special thanks to: Joseph Kelly, Laura Bulbeck, Polly Prior and Chelsea Edwards.

11 13 15 14 12
1 3 5 7 9 10 8 6 4 2

This edition first published 2011 by
FLAME TREE PUBLISHING
Crabtree Hall, Crabtree Lane
Fulham, London SW6 6TY
United Kingdom

www.flametreepublishing.com

Flame Tree Publishing is part of The Foundry Creative Media Co. Ltd

ISBN 978-1-84786-719-3

A CIP record for this book is available from the British Library upon request.

Many thanks to the following for supplying images: **Blackmoor Fruit Nursery/www.blackmoor.co.uk:** 213, 214, 217t, 221l, 223b; **Pure Modern/www.puremodern.co.uk:** 82t, 82b, 90; (HAXNICKS) www.haxnicks.co.uk: 13, 19, 51, 122, 123b, 187b.

Courtesy of **Fotolia** and © the following photographers: Paula Fisher 249. ©iStockphoto.com: /Kelly Cline 8; /James Whittaker 67; /JamesWhittaker/Richard Clark 112, 115b; /audaxi 123t; /makaid/makai dunne 160. Courtesy of **Shutterstock** and © the following photographers: marilyn barbone 1c & 226t, 228t & 252b, 228b, 229b; Susan Fox 3 & 70; macka 4l & 16r; Diana Taliun 4br & 28r; Photoanatomy 4tl & 54r; Mona Makela 5bl & 101r, 205t; mates 5r & 74r, 96; elena moiseeva 6t & 127r; BHJ 6r & 151r; Kiselev Andrey Valerevich 6b & 175r; Pixelbliss 7l & 209r; ˜vvetc˜ 7r & 237r; c.byatt-norman 9 & 111, 52; Connie Wade 10; Eky Studio 11; Marina Nabatova 12r; Thomas M Perkins 12l; Josef Bosak 14; Peter Dean 18; sruenkam 20t; David Fowler 20b, 219; AndiPu 22l; Vitalij Lang 22r; Piotr Marcinski 23; andriscam 25b; Vibrant Image Studio 25t; Chris leachman 26t, 138; ARENA Creative 26b; Konstantin Chagin 30; Lisa F. Young 31, 196; Sebastian Duda 32; Anne Kitzman 33, 88, 205b; Sklep Spozywczy 34r; Tamara Kulikova 34l; David Hughes 35l; Multiart 35r; Claus Mikosch 36; Ingrid Balabanova 37; Olga Lipatova 38; Dan Clausen 39; stocksnapp 40, 69; kamilpetran 42; LianeM 43, 80, 109, 114, 119t, 246; Ilya D. Gridnev 44; Christopher Elwell 45, 190t; ; walshphotos 46; Tiut Vlad 49; pls 50; Gregory Johnston 56, 89, 130, 234; Renate Micallef 57; Monkey Business Images 58; Natalia Aggiato 59; joingate 60; Rosamund Parkinson 61; printzell 62; sydeen 63; Lelde J-R 64; Robert Hackett 65; Graeme Dawes 66; ason 68; R-photos 73; emin kuliyev 76r; Theresa Martinez 76l; Margaret M Stewart 77; Sally Scott 78; 6377724229 79; Carolina K. Smith, M.D. 81t; Joy Brown 81b; Ruslana Stovner 83; Brandon Blinkenberg 84l, 164; KAppleyard 84r; Kelly Richardson 85; Awardimages 86; Victor I. Makhankov 87; ncn18 92; Caroline RW 93t; nice_pictures 93b; tim elliott 94; Tim Bird 95; miskolin 97; Stefan Fierros 103t, 186, 198; Garsya 103b; Richard Griffin 104r; Karen Kaspar 104l; Copit 105; Anest 106; Olena Simko 107; saiko3p 108; Foxy 110; Elena Elisseeva 113; psv 115t; sarka 116; Vera Dolezalova 117; Oleg Kozlov 119b; Graphic design 120; Petr Jilek 121; Menna 128; Portokalis 129; Henrik Larsson 130; Beata Becla 131; Olga Miltsova 132; Sasha Davas 134; Andi Berger 135, 203b; Payless Images 136; Patricia Hofmeester 137, 139; Boleslaw Kubica 140t; Pasta 140b; marilyn barbone 141; jason aron 142; Shebeko 143; Evgenia Bolyukh 144; AdamEdwards 145t; Shawn Hempel 145b, 232; Brian A Jackson 146; mundoview 147; John Bloor 148; Dariusz Majgier 152; Larisa Lofitskaya 153; Bruce MacQueen 154b; pwrmc 154t; epsylon_lyrae 155; Steven Paul Pepper 156b, 190b; joyfuldesigns 156t, 242; mashe 158t; tepic 158b; Suto Norbert Zsolt 159t; Vladimir Chernyanskiy 159b; Yusia 161b; Margarita Borodina 162l; humpkin 166; mik ulyannikov 167; Matthew Stansfield 168; discpicture 169; dusan964 170; Daniel Prudek 171; Catalin Petolea 172; Meryll 176; Tereza Dvorak 177; Argunova 178t; Nelstudio 178b; Valentyn Volkov 179; Pavelk 180; surabhi25 181; Lilyana Vynogradova 182; David Woolfenden 183; Elnur 184; David Burrows 187t; Larry Korb 189t; Sally Wallis 189b; Annavee 191; Verbenko 193; Anna Sedneva 194; Newton Page 195; BKingFoto 197t; Denis and Yulia Pogostins 197b, 221r; Alexander Bark 200; krivenko 201; C. Rene Ammundsen 202b; David Scheuber 202t; Joerg Beuge 204l; Nousha 204r; Robyn Mackenzie 206; Gina Rothfels 210; pjhpix 211l; Vilor 211r; nanadou 215; Bertl123 216; Jason L. Price 217b; gosphotodesign 218; Krzysztof Slusarczyk 220; yuris 222; sharon kingston 223t; Juriah Mosin 224; marina ljubanovic 225; inacio pires 226b; c. 227; mayer kleinostheim 229t; Marie C Fields 230; June Marie Sobrito 231; Lessadar 233b; ShopArtGallery 233t; Sharon Day 238; toriru 240; Jen Phillips 241; April Cat 243; RTimages 244; w.g.design 247; Fedorov Oleksiy 250. Courtesy of **Wikicommons** and used under the following licence: http://commons.wikimedia.org/wiki/Commons:GNU_Free_Documentation_License_1.2: Snowmanradio 41; Karsten Dörre 157; A13ean 161t; Rasbak 162r; Dollymoon 165.

GREEN GUIDES

Crops in Pots

RACHELLE STRAUSS

Foreword by PIPPA GREENWOOD

FLAME TREE
PUBLISHING

Contents

Foreword **8**

Introduction **10**

Joys of Container Gardening **16**

Just because you may not have a traditional vegetable plot does not mean you should miss out on the thrill and satisfaction of growing your own food. This chapter shows that container gardening is accessible to anyone, regardless of age or physical ability. The food you grow will rack up no air or road miles from pot to plate, so is good for the environment, too. And best of all, you will enjoy the can't-be-beaten taste of freshly picked produce straight from your garden.

Getting Started **28**

Container gardening does require some input, and it pays to think in advance about what you will need. This chapter will help with the planning process. You should take into account your budget, the amount of growing space available to you, the light requirements of your plants, and the need for good-quality compost, suitable gardening materials and an accessible water supply for your burgeoning crops.

What to Grow **54**

This is an important chapter. As a first-time or enthusiastic gardener, it is easy to become carried away and grow things that are not part of your food repertoire. While it is great to experiment, it is best to plan what to plant around what you really eat and what you have the time and space to grow. This way you will save money and ensure you have a ready supply of produce to supplement your weekly menu. Skim through at your peril!

Preparing to Grow **74**

Before embarking on your growing bonanza, you will need all the basics: pots and containers; seeds; tools; and compost. In this chapter, we run through the pros and cons of the different sorts of gardening kit available to ensure you buy only what is necessary and best suited to your growing space and requirements. There is also an outline of the gardening year, helping you see what to expect from your garden and what your garden expects from you, season to season.

How to Grow **100**

After all the preparation, this is where you can finally get stuck in. In this chapter, we give you straightforward, practical advice about when to plant, how to sow your seed, how to care for your seedlings, how to know when to transplant, hardening off, planting out, feeding and watering. We also show you how you can lengthen your growing season through the use of cloches, polytunnels, fleeces or blankets.

Harvesting **126**

If you have followed the advice given so far, you should be faced with the delicious prospect of harvesting the fruits of your labours. We show you how to tell when your crop is ready and how to store it either short-term or for leaner times of the year. We also help you deal with gluts, either by successive sowing or preserving your produce by freezing, dehydrating or turning into chutney.

Pests & Problems **150**

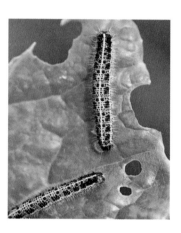

Any garden, even on a small scale, has its particular problems. These can range from pests such as slugs, ladybirds and snails to blight, mildew and weeds. This chapter deals with most of the problems you are likely to encounter in a container garden and gives possible preventions (quality compost, companion planting) and possible cures (cleaning pots, removing debris). These good gardening habits should stop most trouble in its tracks.

Vegetables & Salads **174**

This is where we get into specifics. We give you the low-down on the veg and salad that is best suited to a container garden, and the particular varieties you should look out for. As well as giving ideas and inspiration, the chapter gives you top tips on how to grow specific crops, the conditions they require and how to care for them. Even if you are a complete novice, there will be something here that you can grow.

Fruits, Herbs & Edible Flowers 208

If you are limited for space, it is easy to disregard fruit as a potential crop, but this chapter will show you that it is quite possible to have a successful mini-orchard so long as you choose the right varieties. And herbs and edible flowers are useful as well as beautiful. They are easy to grow, abundant in the right conditions, will give flavour and colour to your food and also attract valuable pollinators to the garden.

Frugal Gardening 236

If you are interested in container gardening but not so thrilled at the thought of parting with your cash, this is the chapter for you. These days we are all encouraged to reduce, reuse and recycle, which is a maxim that can be applied to gardening. You will save money and help the environment by growing your own anyway, but if you can grow your own using (free) swapped seed, homemade compost and wooden crates from your local greengrocer, so much the better. This chapter will give you tips and ideas on how you can get the most for your garden out of spending the least.

Further Reading 252

Websites 253

Index 254

Foreword

Growing your own food is something that it is easy to become passionate about, and I am! There is nothing to beat the incredible feeling you have when you realize that a good percentage of the food on the table originates from your own plot, and was grown by you – raised from a small plant, or perhaps just a sprinkling of seeds, and then fed and watered until that wonderful day when the crops were first ready to harvest. Food growing really produces the best feel-good factor I know!

'Growing your own' is getting more and more popular, with the more obvious benefits being something lots of people are really starting to enjoy – fresh crops growing close to the house, and the simply wonderful taste and texture of home grown – often converting those less inclined to eat vegetables to actually enjoy all that the myriad of different crops has to offer. Growing your own vegetables also means less environmental impact with zero food miles and, for those who garden organically, zero use of pesticides. But it is also very convenient, as you can have a plentiful supply of your favourite vegetables close to hand.

For those with smaller gardens, or gardens consisting largely of paved areas, growing your own may seem out of the question. Not so! The vast majority of the more commonly grown crops can easily be grown in good-sized containers. These can be smart new ones or simply cleaned-up recycled containers – almost anything will do as long as it is a decent size and adequately supplied with drainage holes. So if you have more of a back yard than a garden, or perhaps are even restricted to balcony gardening, there are plenty of opportunities to grow vegetables, herbs and even some fruit. Crops in pots can also be the best solution if, like me, your soil is very heavy and well supplied with chunks of rock – a good, deep container full of compost mixed with sieved garden soil is the only way I can grow a good looking and half decent crop of carrots or parsnips!

I love growing my own crops and would encourage anyone to have a go. I was brought up growing vegetables and learned just what to do from my mother, a wonderful and very keen gardener. Learning like that is easy, as you absorb the knowledge and techniques effortlessly and in the company of someone who really knows what to do and when to do it. But if you were not that fortunate, then a well-planned and illustrated book with plenty of information in a digestible form is great. In this book you will find a bountiful supply of good, practical information and ideas to make growing crops in containers more straightforward and rewarding than you might ever have thought possible. So, have a read, get inspired and get growing your own fruit, vegetables and herbs. You won't look back, I'm sure !

Pippa Greenwood
Gardening expert, author and broadcaster

Introduction

Have you ever looked longingly at a friend's garden and wished you had a bigger space? Would you like to grow your own food but lack the time to manage a vegetable plot? Would you like to save money, reduce your 'food miles' and improve your health? Then container gardening is for you!

A Popular Choice

Growing vegetables in pots is becoming increasingly popular. Many people have small gardens or none at all and are juggling careers, family schedules and other commitments. Contrary to popular belief, you can feed yourself well from crops grown solely in containers. Most crops will survive in pots as long as the container is big enough and they get enough light, water and nutrients.

Benefits

There are many benefits to be gained from growing your own food in containers. You'll be able to reduce food miles, reduce packaging and food waste, enjoy fresh, seasonal produce and get gentle exercise while tending to your plants. In addition you'll spend time outdoors in the fresh air sowing seeds, watering and harvesting your crops.

Going Green

By growing some of your own food, you can use specially selected pest control and fertilizers, or try your hand at organic or biodynamic gardening. This has huge benefits for the environment such as attracting useful insects to your garden, reducing chemical run-off into the land and rivers and minimizing harm to wildlife.

Reducing Waste

By growing your food in containers, you'll be able to step outside your door and pick your own lunch! There will be no packaging to dispose of afterwards, you'll be able to eat fresh food for a few pence and, because you pick exactly the amount you need, wastage is automatically reduced.

Healthy Lifestyle

Eating fresh, seasonal food is one of the keys to good health and wellbeing and growing your own is one way to achieve this. You will be able to:

- Eat fresh, seasonal food on a daily basis.
- Increase your intake of organic food for less money.
- Increase the amount of time you spend in the fresh air.
- Reduce stress and tension by tending to your plants.
- Achieve the recommended 'five-a-day' portions of fruit and vegetables.
- Get maximum nutrition, vitamins and minerals from your food.

Exercise

There are numerous health benefits to getting outdoors every day. Many people work long hours in offices. When they get home there are chores to do, gyms to go to, children to be taxied around and then most people just want to collapse in front of the television. By taking care of a few containers of crops you'll be more tempted to get outside each day and enjoy some fresh air.

Who Can Grow Crops in Pots?

The wonderful thing about container gardening is that it is accessible to all. People with disabilities who find it hard to bend, dig or kneel can enjoy gardening by sitting down at the side of a raised bed. Young children can take care of their own containers, the elderly may gain tremendous satisfaction from growing food and for busy people with time constraints, container gardening reduces stress and increases success.

People with Small Spaces

With containers a whole new world of gardening is opened up for people who don't have a garden! You can grow salad plants, vegetables, herbs and fruit on a balcony, roof garden or patio, or in window boxes. You can utilize the space available by choosing anything from plastic pots bought at a garden centre to old sinks! If you have no available ground space, try hanging baskets and wall planters or grow food indoors.

People with Limited Time

For busy people, taking care of a few pots of food is a great way to balance a hectic lifestyle. You can plant as few containers as you wish and spend just five minutes a day gardening if this fits in with your plans. When your confidence or time increases you can add more containers and choose more challenging plants to grow.

Making Gardening Simple

Using containers is much less overwhelming and time consuming than tending to an allotment or traditional vegetable plot. You can choose fuss free plants such as herbs or salad leaves to begin with and gradually build up to plants which need more time and care. Children can easily grow their own food in containers because they don't have to do heavy digging or pull out weeds with long roots.

Reaping Benefits

Growing food in crops has several advantages over traditional gardening, for example weeds cannot establish good roots so you'll spend less time weeding. With a pot you can easily get the soil pH and condition just as you need it. And instead of renting an allotment, which involves travel and cost, you can just step outside and get straight on with your gardening.

Containing Growth

Some crops are invasive in the ground; by containing the plant in a pot you can stop them taking over. You can grow fruit bushes in pots to prevent them getting unwieldy and direct the growing energy into the fruit rather than foliage. Weeds won't be able to take over if you change the soil regularly in your containers.

Food All Year Round

By growing food in pots you can extend your growing season. Soil will warm up quicker and you can protect containers or move them around to take advantage of sunlight. In the winter containers can be covered or brought indoors to protect them from frost damage.

About this Book

This book tells you all you need to know about growing food in containers. If you have limited space, time or abilities or have had disasters in a traditional vegetable plot there are plenty of tips and tricks to get you on the road to success. You'll soon be harvesting your own food and inviting friends over for a home grown meal!

What Will You Learn?

You'll discover that growing your own food can be easy and rewarding. You'll find out all you've wanted to know about the best foods to grow in containers, the easiest ones to take care of and how to harvest them. You'll find out how to deal with pests and make the most of your harvest.

You will also find out:

- How to use containers for growing food.
- What sorts of pots you can use.
- How to gain maximum food from minimum space.
- How to grow food without a garden.
- How to choose the right compost, fertilizer and tools.
- When to sow your seeds.
- How to harvest and preserve your food.
- How to deal with pests.
- Detailed instructions on what to grow.

Checklist

Keep the following in mind when planning your container garden:

☑ **Why grow crops?** What is your incentive to grow food in containers – is it limited space, time or money? Or do you want to improve your health or help the environment?

☑ **Food waste**: How much food do you throw away each week?

☑ **Packaging**: How much food packaging do you discard each week?

☑ **Organic issues**: Do you want to grow organically or conventionally?

☑ **Which crops?** What do your neighbours and friends grow successfully?

☑ **Space**: How much space can you dedicate to pots and containers?

☑ **Recycling**: What do you have at home that could be used to grow food in?

☑ **Time**: How much time are you prepared to spend looking after your containers?

☑ **Schedule**: When would you like to start gardening: today, next week, next month or next season? How about right now?

The Joys of Container Gardening

Any Time, Any Place

You might be wondering why you really want to grow food in pots. You might be looking at your tiny patch of land, or even your balcony and thinking it's not possible. However I think you'll agree that the satisfaction of being able to grow and harvest some of your own food and the delight of watching plants push their way through the soil is worth it. Not to mention a constant supply of fresh food!

Space Saving

However restricted or awkward your space is, there will be a way to make it productive. Using containers is ideal for small spaces; it's like having a mini garden to work with and you can grow a large variety of fruit, vegetables, herbs and edible flowers in the tiniest of spaces which will look as good as it tastes.

Small Spaces

Whether you have a rooftop garden, a small piece of decking, a window box, some hanging baskets, a patio or only room for grow bags, you'll be able to grow your own food. If you live in a high-rise apartment with a balcony you can also enjoy a little self-sufficiency. You can even grow food on windowsills inside your home. You really don't need a garden at all!

Food Glorious Food

Food can be grown virtually anywhere. By using containers you can open up the tiniest plot for crops. Here are some spaces in which you can grow food:

- ✅ **Rooftop gardens**
- ✅ **Balconies**
- ✅ **Decking**
- ✅ **Courtyards**
- ✅ **Window boxes**
- ✅ **Windowsills**
- ✅ **Hanging baskets**
- ✅ **Small patios**
- ✅ **Raised beds**

Convenience

If the thought of travelling to an allotment after a busy day at work puts you off, imagine being able to step outside your door and find pots of food waiting for you. You can pick what you need when you need it plus your gardening can take as little as a couple of hours a week once your plants are established. You can also grow just one or two crops to try, whereas traditional gardening is done in long rows and you often end up with a glut you can't use.

Secrets to Success

If your crops are easily accessible and right outside your door, your chances of successful growing are much higher. It's often an 'out of sight, out of mind' attitude or the fact the allotment is a couple of miles away that leads to failure during the growing season. By having your pots close to hand you'll be enjoying some home grown food in no time.

Did You Know?

860,000 tonnes of fresh vegetables and salad are thrown away every year – why not grow your own and reduce food waste!

Ground Control

A major benefit of container gardening is that you have more control over your growing environment. Instead of being stuck with an allotment containing poor quality soil, a waterlogged garden or a shady patch, you can choose and maintain your soil condition, keep pots free draining and move them around to benefit from more sunshine or shade.

Invasive Growers

Some plants, such as mint, are invasive and will take over if put into the ground. It is an aggressive plant and will spread across an entire plot if left unchecked. By growing mint in a pot you can keep it where you want it and prevent it taking nutrients from the soil which can leave other plants struggling to survive.

Other crops, such as courgettes, will take up masses of room in an allotment or open plot of ground. You'll find that small courgettes will turn into large marrows virtually overnight! By keeping the roots contained in a large container or grow bag you'll be able to enjoy smaller crops with more flavour throughout the season.

Pest Control

It is easier to spot and deal with pests in containers and you have a much better chance of preventing them spreading to other plants. If you keep your garden small and are able to see the plants easily because they are up off the ground, then you'll be more likely to spot pests and prevent damage before it occurs.

Diseases

Diseases are less likely to take hold in container crops. Firstly, using potting soil reduces the risk of distributing organisms that spread diseases via contaminated soil. Secondly your crops are easier to see and you can take swift action if any damage occurs. You can get on eye level with plants in containers, so you can spot diseases and prevent them spreading!

Weather Conditions

If the weather suddenly turns cold or there is a prolonged hot, dry spell you can move your plants around if they are in containers. It's easy to orient crops in pots to an ideal position for their optimal growth because with smaller containers you can move the whole lot. For larger containers, the soil is easier to dig in order to move plants to another spot.

Growing Season

You can protect containers far better than open soil so you can easily extend your growing season. By carefully insulating pots with old bubble wrap or blankets and keeping containers close to your home you can keep their soil warmer than ground soil. During a harsh winter you can also bring small pots indoors for added protection.

Did You Know?

Rice husk pots can be added to the compost heap and will rot down with the rest of the garden waste.

Accessible Gardening

If hard digging, bending over to pull up weeds, kneeling to tend to plants or rigorous pruning is too difficult then container gardening can provide the perfect solution. You can grow exactly the amount you want and keep your garden at levels which are easy to maintain. If you have physical disabilities, you can tailor your pots to suit your requirements by elevating containers or using raised beds. Removing weeds is easier because you can get to them before they establish deep roots.

Family Time

Container gardening is a great activity for the whole family. Children can take care of herbs or a quick-growing crop such as radishes. Elderly people can keep their garden a manageable size. Novices can start with one or two crops and build it up. Busy professionals can maintain a small edible garden to fit around other commitments.

Quality Food

Once of the best health benefits of growing crops is the ability to pick fresh, seasonal food any day of the year. It's much easier to eat your 'five a day' portions of fruit and vegetables if it's outside your door. In addition you'll be motivated to get outside every day for some fresh air. The feel-good factor of learning a new skill, tending to something and being self-sufficient are very important to health and well-being.

Save Money and Go Green

There's never been a better time to grow some of your own food. With food prices rising and more and more people becoming concerned about economic issues, growing food is one way to contribute something valuable to your health, bank balance and environment. Mortgage rates, rent and council tax use up a big proportion of household income, so finding ways to spend less on food can extend your budget.

Reduce Your Food Bills

There are many ways to make growing food a frugal activity; not only do you save money on buying food, but there are health and social benefits too. When you consider 15 per cent of the average household income is spent on food, there are big opportunities to save money by growing your own. Admittedly, food costs comparatively less than it did a few decades ago, but eating 'value' lines and cheap processed food may come at a cost to our health and environment.

Did You Know?

According to the Food and Agriculture Organization of the United Nations, global food prices will go on rising and could be 20 per cent higher in the next 10 years.

Avoiding Waste

If you consider the average household throws away one third of the food bought, this means one third of the money you spend is being wasted. Imagine being able to save one third of your food bill! In the UK, it is estimated that this amounts to £10.2 billion of avoidable food waste every year. In the US, household food waste adds up to a staggering $43 billion.

Advantages of Container Gardening

Hopefully by now you'll realize some of the wonderful benefits of growing crops in pots and containers. Here's a recap:

- **Excellent for restricted spaces.**
- **Convenient – right outside your door.**
- **Keeps aggressive plants in check.**
- **Suitable for all levels of fitness.**
- **Simple to deal with pests and diseases.**
- **Can transform spaces into beautiful areas.**
- **You can extend the growing season.**
- **Engages the whole family.**

Environmental Issues

One of the best reasons for growing your own food is reducing environmental impact. Many people are concerned about food miles, pesticides, side effects of intensive farming and excess food packaging. By growing your own food you can take back some responsibility and help protect the environment at the same time.

Food Miles

Food miles is a term which refers to the distance food travels from the farm where it is produced to the kitchen in which it is consumed. It is estimated that the average individual food

travels 1,500 to 2,500 miles from farm to plate. So if you buy a tin of vegetable soup with eight different ingredients in it, it may have travelled 16,000 miles before it reaches your table. A sobering thought.

Reducing Mileage

Buying local, seasonal food reduces air miles. What better way to have zero air miles than stepping outside your back door to find food! As we sit down to eat, few of us consider how far our food has travelled to arrive on our plate. Even food produced in your own country will travel hundreds of miles before it's ready to be eaten.

Transporting Food

Food transportation makes up around 25 per cent of all Heavy Goods Vehicle activity on the roads, contributing to traffic congestion, noise and air pollution; not to mention increased carbon dioxide emissions. The overall environmental impact of food transport doesn't stop once you're back at home with your shopping. Packaging and food waste has to be taken to landfill where it adds more burden to the environment.

Top Tip

Conserve water by installing a water butt or reusing dish water to water your plants.

Food Packaging

In the UK, the volume of food packaging waste each week is equivalent to 245 jumbo jets. By growing some of your own food, you can be part of the solution to waste food packaging. Although a certain amount of packaging is needed to keep food fresh and prevent spoilage, some is excessive and can be avoided. Once in landfill, some materials such as plastic take hundreds of years to decompose, while landfill itself produces greenhouse gases which contribute to climate change.

Reducing Food Waste

Every year, the average householder throws away around one third of the food they buy. Much of this is fresh produce that goes off before it is used. By growing some of your own food in pots you can pick what you need when you need it. This reduces the risk of produce going off before you can use it up.

Here are some reasons why people throw food away:

- **Cooking too much that it gets left in the saucepan.**
- **Serving too much that it gets left on the plate.**
- **Not using food on time and leaving it to go off before it is used.**
- **Changing plans and getting a takeaway or eating something else.**
- **Forgetting what food is in the fridge, cupboard, vegetable rack or fruit bowl.**
- **Forgetting to chill or freeze something in time.**
- **Lack of confidence or knowledge in using up leftovers.**

Checklist

Remember: No matter how small your plot there will be a way to grow your own food.

Accessible: Growing food in containers makes gardening accessible to everyone regardless of physical ability, time constraints or finances.

Control: Growing food in containers offers you more control over your growing environment.

Space: Whether you have a rooftop garden, balcony, small courtyard or a few hanging baskets there will be a way for you to grow some food!

Convenient: Growing food in containers near your home is convenient and you're more likely to take good care of it.

Pests: It's simpler to eliminate pests and diseases when growing food in containers because it's easier to see and deal with them.

Benefits: Growing your own food is better for the environment, can save you money and benefits your health.

Environment: You can choose to grow organically, or use limited pesticides, herbicides and insecticides to lessen your impact on the environment.

Crops to grow: Start thinking about some of the fresh foods you buy regularly; this will give you clues about the sort of crops you might like to grow.

Getting
Started

Planning

We've looked at the benefits of growing your own food in containers and learned that no matter how small your plot, there will be a way for you to enjoy a little self-sufficiency. Now it's time to take a look at your plot in more detail and start designing the way your garden can work for you to ensure maximum success.

Good Planning

There are several things to take into account when planning your garden layout. The most important one is probably your budget. Unlike people with a traditional plot you don't have a free area of land to work on; you need to create your garden from scratch. This will mean buying containers, compost, tools, seeds and fertilizer. How much money can you put aside to set up your garden?

Budgeting

If your budget is limited, there are lots of ways to make your money work harder! The most obvious choice is with containers. Later on you'll discover lots of creative recycling ideas which

won't cost you anything. If you have an unlimited budget then you can choose exactly the right containers for your space, but it's still good to avoid costly mistakes and get value for money.

Shop Around

Spend some time browsing online stores and local garden centres to get ideas of pricing.

Containers come in a variety of materials and styles that vary tremendously in cost. Plastic is usually the cheapest option whereas stone containers are often much more expensive. You'll find all sorts of ornate pots and materials that can be painted to create a stylized look.

Fertilizers

Crops grown in pots are more reliant on you for good watering and the right nutrition. You'll need to feed regularly during the growing season and you'll notice there are different types of fertilizers available. Familiarize yourself with the different brands and types. See if there are any multipurpose fertilizers and estimate how much you think you will need for the amount of crops you want to grow. Add this ongoing cost to your budget.

Seeds

Surprisingly seeds can vary in price too. To keep costs down seeds can be shared with friends and once you start growing you can save your own seeds each year. You may choose to support heritage varieties which tend to cost more, although some environmental charities offer heritage seeds for free. You might prefer more unusual varieties or want to have a go at exotic crops.

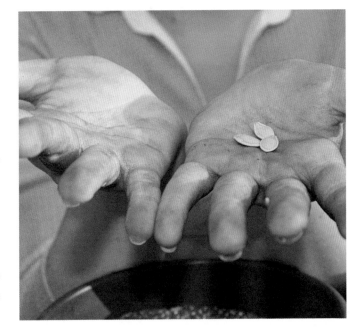

Tools

You'll need a few tools for successful container gardening such as a good hand fork and/or trowel, a watering can with rose attachment or a hosepipe and some gardening gloves. You may find secateurs handy and a potting trowel useful. You tend to get what you pay for, so it's worth spending the most you can afford on tools, even when starting out.

Top Tip

Cut the bottom few inches from an empty 2 litre plastic water bottle, punch a few holes in and use to sow seeds.

Space to Grow

How much space you have will determine how much food you can grow. Clearly some large crops such as Brussels sprouts (which need to be firmly bedded in soil) are not suitable for pots, but you can grow some small fruit trees and many other types of crop. Your varieties will be limited by the amount of space you have to site containers and the size of the containers themselves.

Patios and Roof Gardens

Perhaps you have a small patio or roof garden. These are some of the best areas for container gardening. You can fill the space with containers, raised beds and planters of all shapes and sizes and make use of the ground by using growbags. You can design the garden layout easily to make maximum use of light and space. Don't forget to leave room around the containers so you can get to them easily and remember that roof gardens often provide very little shade, so choose sun-loving crops.

Balconies

The most important thing to bear in mind when using balconies is the weight of the containers when full of soil. You will need to make sure you do not overload the balcony or damage the structure of it. Some balconies have built-in fire escapes which must not be obstructed and there may be legal implications if your balcony is shared. Make sure you are within your legal rights before creating a garden on a balcony.

No Garden or Balcony?

Do you live in a high-rise apartment or a terraced house with no garden? In this case you need to look up instead of down! A few hanging baskets can be used to grow herbs, tumbling tomatoes and trailing edible flowers. You can attach wall planters to the outside of a wall and plant salads or smaller 'baby' vegetables. Be aware that if you live in a listed building you may need permission to attach things to the walls.

Window Boxes

Outdoors, on a south-facing windowsill, you can grow herbs, salads and some baby vegetables. Growing in a window box works especially well if your boxes are outside the kitchen! If you're not able to grow outdoors for some reason (perhaps your home is rented and your landlord will not allow you to attach window boxes) then there is *still* a way for you to grow your own food!

Windowsills

If all else fails and there is no outdoor space for you at all, then you can grow some crops inside. Most Mediterranean crops such as tomatoes and peppers will thrive indoors on a sunny windowsill. Crops grown indoors are less likely to be forgotten or neglected and they can bring a homely feel to your house as well as providing you with food. Herbs can be grown on a kitchen windowsill and picked as you need them.

Conservatories

A conservatory can be used just like a greenhouse! In a small conservatory you can build a long shelf to act like a windowsill to grow peppers, chillies and other plants that like a lot of heat. On the floor you can grow tomatoes in growbags and allow them to grow tall by supporting them with canes or a trellis. A conservatory is a great way to make maximum use of available sunlight.

Up, Down and Sideways

If ground space is limited you're going to need to think outside the box. It might be that you need some large rectangular containers or raised beds on the ground with a platform above for growbags to make maximum use of limited space. You can grow shade lovers in the shadow of sun lovers such as allowing kale to grow underneath beans.

Vertical Gardening

Vertical gardening is very important when you don't have a large surface area. Broad beans, runner beans, peas, courgettes, tomatoes and baby squash grow really well with support. You can either put these in containers and support them with canes or you can build a structure from wood and put netting across to allow plants to clamber and climb across it.

Top Tip

During the summer, take a few stems of your favourite herbs, tie them in bunches and dry indoors ready for winter use.

Square Foot Gardening

By utilizing square foot gardening, you can increase your yield in a small space. Simply divide your space up into square foot areas (buying pots which measure a square foot is ideal) and plant either one, four, nine or 16 plants, depending on their size in each square foot. For example you would plant one basil plant, four lettuces, nine spinach plants or 16 carrots in one square foot.

Doorsteps

Do you only have a south-facing front doorstep? Then put a couple of containers on it and grow some food! You could plant a large container either side of your front door with herbs or salad for daily picking. Add a couple of hanging baskets of tomatoes and you've got salad throughout the summer. Put a window box along the front window of your home for some edible flowers and you'll have a colourful and healthy meal ready to eat. Attach a planter to the wall for strawberries and you can enjoy a delicious pudding too!

Recap on Utilizing Space

Hopefully this will have given you some ideas about making your small space work for you. Have a think about the following ways in which you could grow food:

- Small patios are ideal for container gardens – grow to fill your space!
- Roof gardens are good too; remember to check the weight of your filled pots if using roof space.
- Balconies make great spaces for containers; first assess weight limits and make sure you don't block fire escapes.
- No garden? You can attach hanging baskets or wall planters to the outside of your home.
- Window boxes are ideal if you live in a high-rise apartment and don't have access to outdoors.
- Make use of indoor windowsills for heat-loving crops.
- Do you have a sunny conservatory? Turn it into a productive 'greenhouse'.
- Garden upwards instead of sideways – raised beds on the ground with growbags suspended on a shelf above is a good way to maximize growing space.
- If you don't have ground space, look upwards; climbing plants are ideal.
- Could you utilize square foot gardening principles to maximize your yield?
- Do you have a doorstep where you could put planters?

Light Conditions

The most important requirement for all plants is sunshine. The correct amount of light is the difference between a substantial crop and a major flop! Although you can grow most things in a limited space, you cannot grow anything without sunshine. The first thing to do is spend a few days tracking the sun around the space you want to grow food and see if you get enough light for a successful harvest.

Sunlight

Most crops need a minimum of eight hours sunshine each day. It might be that part of your plot gets sunshine, in which case this is the area to plan your vegetable garden. Some vegetables and herbs will tolerate a bit of shade and these can be planted in partially shady areas but most crops need full sun during the growing season to survive. If the amount of space that gets sunlight is very limited you might need to be creative about maximizing use of that space.

Sun and Shade

Orientate your design to make the best use of the available sunny areas in your garden and take time to find out what conditions your chosen crops can tolerate. When tracking available hours of sunlight you'll need to bear in mind any shadows that structures or tall plants might cause. Make sure you don't opt for tall crops such as runner beans and then discover they cast too much shadow over the rest of the crops.

Sun Lovers

Plants which bear fruit such as peppers, tomatoes and cucumbers need the most sunlight. Mediterranean herbs such as basil require a lot of sun too. Root crops such as radishes, beetroot and onions can stand more shade than fruit growing crops. Leafy crops such as kale, lettuce and spinach can tolerate more shade than most. Some herbs such as mint can tolerate partial shade. Bear these patterns in mind when working out which foods you would like to grow.

Optimizing Light

You've learned that most crops need eight hours of sunlight to thrive. Have a think about the following when planning your gardening area:

- Could you use reflective materials or paint a wall white to gain maximum light?
- Spend a few days tracking the sun around your chosen area – does it get full or partial sun?
- Write a list of your favourite foods and see if they require full sun or can tolerate some shade.
- Think about shadows – are there tall structures that could obscure sunlight?

Top Tip

Think about ways to reuse water – save it when cleaning out the fish tank, emptying out paddling pools or from an air conditioning unit.

Soil

If you are growing exclusively in containers it's not advisable to use garden soil. Although it is free, garden soil has limited nutrients, can be contaminated with weed seeds and compacts quickly which means your crops will not thrive. In addition, using garden soil increases the risk of spreading pests and diseases. You'll need to get hold of some good quality compost to fill your containers instead.

Healthy Soil

Soil is a living ecosystem. On a large expanse of land, soil is pretty much self-regulating as long as you don't deplete it. Worms and micro-organisms keep soil healthy, the addition of compost enriches the soil while leaves and plant matter decay into the earth providing nutrients for future growth. In small containers, it is not possible to maintain 'living soil' so you'll have to use a growing medium that is rich in nutrients and keep feeding it. Remember, healthy soil leads to healthy plants.

Sourcing Compost

When browsing a garden centre for compost, the choice can be overwhelming. There are multipurpose composts, seed compost, ericaceous, peat-free, organic – the list is endless! You might be wondering what the difference is, whether you need different types or will one sort do, or if it's worth paying extra for organic compost. Good compost supports healthy roots and retains enough nutrition and water to sustain growth, without becoming waterlogged.

Make Your Own

If you want to be really self-sufficient and you have some space, making your own compost is the best idea. Not only will you save money but you'll be able to put your old leaves, kitchen peelings and dead plants to good use – in effect you'll be 'closing the loop' in your own back yard. You can buy small compost bins especially designed for small gardens which work very well if located in a warm spot.

Free Compost

Perhaps you have a friend with a large garden or a colleague with an allotment who can give you compost? You could arrange to drop off your kitchen peelings and plant waste in exchange for your share of the compost. Some people offer compost on their local Freecycle group (www.freecycle.org) or you might see it advertised in a local newspaper or shop. People are only too happy to have their compost cleared if they have too much, so it's worth asking around.

Compost from Municipal Waste

In areas where green waste is collected from households, some local authorities sell the resulting compost back to residents. This is a great way to keep things local and help close the loop. The compost made by local authorities varies in quality but is useful as potting compost or for adding nutrients to existing container soil.

Buying Compost

If you need to buy compost then make sure you purchase it from a reputable source. If you can't get hold of locally managed compost you'll have to buy it from a garden centre or nursery. You can bulk buy online from stores and have it delivered to your home. Another idea is to get together with friends and order a bulk bag to share.

For most crops grown in containers you'll need to buy bags of compost – either soil-based or soil-less. Each type has its advantages and disadvantages. When browsing around a garden centre you might find different types of compost for different jobs, but in most cases multipurpose compost will be fine for any type of container and crop.

Soil-based Compost

Soil-based compost contains sterilised good quality loam mixed with peat, sharp sand, lime and fertilizer. Loam is made up of sand, silt and clay in 40-40-20 per cent concentration. While sand, silt and clay make up any type of ordinary garden soil, most have high proportions of either sand or clay and are not ideal. Loam is a perfect balance and composts made from this are ideal for crops that stay in pots permanently such as fruit bushes and trees.

Pros and Cons

There are a few advantages and disadvantages to soil-based compost:

 It holds nutrients well.

 It provides stability for tall plants in pots.

 It keeps plants well anchored.

 It is heavy, so is unsuitable where weight is an issue, such as on a balcony or in hanging baskets.

John Innes

The John Innes Institute has created several soil-based composts with different ratios of ingredients for specific purposes. These are readily available at garden centres and take the guesswork out of buying compost. These composts contain enough plant food for one to two months, depending on the plant and the season. Contrary to popular belief, John Innes is not a brand name but a general formulation; a number of manufacturers produce mixes that bear this title.

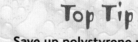

Top Tip

Save up polystyrene packing peanuts for drainage material in the bottom of pots.

The Right Nutrients

Seeds require just a few nutrients otherwise seedlings can 'burn', whereas some full-grown pot plants and crops such as tomatoes require extra nourishment. John Innes Seed Compost has a low level of nutrients while John Innes Composts Nos. 1, 2 and 3 have an increasing amount of nutrients, as the numbers go up. Think of seedlings like babies – you wouldn't give a roast dinner to a six-month-old baby!

Seed or Potting Compost

As the name suggests, potting compost (or seed compost) is ideal for growing almost any type of seed. It contains the right nutrients for early growth and is perfect for seedling trays. Traditional seed compost contains around two parts loam, one part peat and one part sand to allow retention of nutrients but it's free draining to prevent seedlings rotting. John Innes Seed Compost is ideal for virtually all seeds. You can fill a seed tray with seed compost and it will contain enough nutrients for early development of seedlings.

Top Tip

If adding materials to compost, don't make more than you will use over the course of a month.

Which One to Buy?

 John Innes No.1: This has the least amount of fertilizer in it, making it ideal for sowing seeds or potting up young seedlings.

 John Innes No. 2: This has slightly more nutrients so is ideal for potting on when seedlings and young plants need more food. When you are ready to move vegetable plants into medium sized pots, this is the formula to use. No. 2 contains double the amounts of nutrients than No.1 to suit established plants.

 John Innes No. 3: With the most fertilizer, this is used for final potting and permanent container plants. It's suitable for heavy feeders such as the squash family or tomatoes.

 John Innes Ericaceous Compost: Lime free, this is created especially for plants that hate lime and need an acidic environment.

Multipurpose Compost

Multipurpose compost is the most common type and can be sourced easily and cheaply. You can use it for sowing seeds and for potting up and most plants will do well in it. multipurpose compost has enough nutrients in it to give seeds and plants a good start but after about six weeks you'll need to start adding fertilizer. While it is suitable for most crops, not all plants will grow well in it. Some plants, for example blueberries, require very acidic soil; multipurpose compost is too alkaline. Other crops, such as carrots, require soil that drains very quickly; multipurpose compost is too compact and the carrots could rot.

Multipurpose compost can be too alkaline for some plants, such as blueberries.

Top Tip

Going on holiday? Put a few inches of water in a children's paddling pool and stand your potted plants in it.

Growbags

Growbags are ideal for beginners. These are filled with nutritious growing medium; perfect for crops like tomatoes, peppers and salad. They are an economical way to try gardening as you don't need to buy a container. If you have a successful first year and want to expand your gardening, you can mix the spent growbag contents with fresh compost to use in containers the following year.

Soil-less Compost

Soil-less compost is made from peat, or peat substitutes such as coir or bark to which nutrients and fine sand are added. Advantages and disadvantages include:

- It is lightweight.
- Good for hanging baskets and window boxes.
- Dries out quickly and needs more vigilant watering.
- Once it dries out, soil-less compost is difficult to rehydrate.

Peat-based Compost

One of the most popular types of compost is sourced from peat. It is used because it is excellent at holding water and retaining nutrients. Unfortunately, peatland landscapes are being irrevocably damaged by commercial peat extraction. The extent of damage is so great that the UK government has set a target for 90% of the total horticultural market to be peat free.

Peatlands

Peatlands are an important aspect of the environment. Not only are they a natural habitat for many plants and animals but they store carbon. As long as it remains wet and un-decomposed, peat stores significant quantities of the greenhouse gas carbon dioxide (CO_2). Once drained, ploughed or extracted for use in gardens, the process of oxidation speeds up, releasing carbon into the atmosphere and exacerbating the impacts of climate change.

Making a Difference

Over two-thirds of all peat used in British horticulture is used by the amateur gardening market, so you can play a key role in reducing peat usage. With improved alternatives it's not difficult to find another suitable growing medium. With peat-free compost the peat content is replaced by composted barks, coir or other products and these products are readily available.

Peat harvesting near Easkey, Co. Sligo, Ireland.

Ericaceous Compost

Ericaceous compost is especially for plants that love acid and hate alkaline soils. It has more peat than other types and no lime. Any added fertilizers are acidic too.

Which Compost?

Depending on what you want to grow, there are advantages and disadvantages to the different types of compost available. Here's a recap:

Did You Know?

English Heritage estimates that 75 per cent of all peat-land archaeology has been destroyed.

- Soil-based compost is heavy and provides a good base for pots in an exposed site.
- Soil-based compost holds nutrients well.
- Soil-less composts are ideal for hanging baskets and window boxes.
- Peat-free and organic composts are better for the environment.
- multipurpose compost is easy to use and ideal for beginners.
- Ericaceous compost is essential for lime-hating plants such as blueberries.
- Growbags are ideal for beginners and great for plants like tomatoes and salads.
- Soil-based compost is unsuitable for hanging baskets or on balconies.
- Soil-less composts dry out quickly and can be difficult to rehydrate.
- Peat-free compost does not hold onto nutrients well so needs regular feeding.
- Peat-free and organic composts are more expensive to buy.
- Growbags work out relatively expensive for what you get – you pay for convenience.

> ## Did You Know?
> Species such as the orang-utan are threatened by peatland destruction.

Adding Materials

Depending on what you want to grow, you may need loam-based compost or a particularly moisture-retentive mix. You can buy multipurpose compost and then add certain materials to tweak the properties. Adding materials such as perlite or sharp sand increases drainage and is good for sowing seeds. Adding loam makes a heavier mix suitable for long-term planting such as fruit trees.

From left to right: peat, perlite and vermiculite.

Horticultural Grit

Horticultural grit is a natural material derived from rock. It creates spaces within compost to allow good drainage and aeration. It is also useful for top-heavy plants because it adds weight to the compost, improves plant anchorage and does not alter the pH of the compost. Herbs that come from a Mediterranean climate and enjoy stony, well-drained soil will benefit from horticultural grit. Mix three parts grit with seven parts multipurpose compost by volume to lighten the growing medium.

Perlite

Perlite is a man-made product produced from glass which is a lightweight alternative to grit for 'opening up' compost. Mixing perlite into compost is ideal for plants that might get waterlogged during heavy rainfall in the winter. Combine 70 per cent multipurpose compost with 30 per cent perlite by volume. Remember that plants will now be more prone to drought, so keep watering during dry spells.

Vermiculite

Vermiculite is man-made and produced from clay. Vermiculite improves the drainage and water-retaining properties of composts and contains nutrients. Vermiculite helps to inhibit damping off (rotting) of seedlings. Fine vermiculite makes good cover for germinating seedlings as it creates a humid, warm and aerated environment, ideal for germination.

Sand

Sand is a natural material available in a variety of particle sizes. Coarse sand improves drainage whereas fine sand improves the 'wettability' of potting mixes. You should never use builders' sand as it raises the pH of the soil. Always buy horticultural sharp sand which improves drainage and adds weight.

A Weighty Issue

Where weight of soil-based composts would be an issue, such as on a balcony or in hanging baskets and window boxes, you can either buy a soil-less compost or mix equal parts John

Innes No.2 with soil-less multipurpose compost and add 15 per cent by volume of perlite or vermiculite.

Storing Compost

Composts, regardless of type, can deteriorate or change rapidly if stored incorrectly. The most serious changes are in the pH of the product. It is normal for composts to increase in pH, followed by a gradual decrease as organic nitrogen is mineralized. This is normal and natural, but it's advisable to ensure these changes occur as slowly as possible to give plants time to acclimatize.

Storage Tips

Here's how to keep your compost in prime condition:

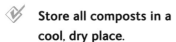

- **Store all composts in a cool, dry place.**
- **Preferably store inside cool buildings such as a garage, away from heat sources.**
- **If storing outside, avoid direct sunlight – a north-facing wall is ideal.**
- **If storing outside keep rain off the product – a porch roof or tarpaulin is ideal.**
- **Minimize heat damage by covering with white plastic sheeting.**
- **Keep bags of compost off the ground – a pallet can help.**
- **When you buy new compost, use the old compost first.**
- **Re-seal a new bag after use to keep contents moist and prevent contamination.**

Layout

Now you've learned about the space you have available, the number of hours of sunlight on your plot and the different types of compost available, it's time to plan the layout of your container garden. Make sure you leave enough room in between containers; if you find you have nowhere to empty and fill pots or you can't get to them when everything is fully grown you'll probably give up.

Sunshine

Hopefully you now know where the sunniest areas are on your plot. You might have south-facing walls which can be utilized to their fullest. Perhaps you have a south-facing patio. On the other hand you might have to contend with partial shade which will reduce the types of crops you can grow. You might be able to increase light with the use of reflective materials or taking down structures that cast shadows.

Take Growth into Account

A plot can look very different when empty containers are placed on it compared to the height of the growing season. Remember your plants will grow sideways as well as upwards, so ensure you leave plenty of space in between pots for growth and for you to get around. You need to be able to water, weed and harvest and plants need room to thrive. If they are too cramped they can die. Some plants like to sprawl sideways or snake along the ground; take all this into account before sowing your first seeds.

Support Systems

Growing food in containers can take more initial setting up than in an open plot. If you're growing climbing crops such as beans you'll need sturdy support for the plants to take hold of and climb. You'll need containers that are robust enough to withstand heavy gusts of wind when they have tall plants in them and supports that can stay upright in bad weather. Lightweight plastic containers are no good if you live in an area that is exposed to high winds. You might consider growing more tender plants or those which you use regularly closer to your back door so you can keep an eye on them.

Sustainable Planting

Consider the permaculture idea too where plants are grown for the support they can give one another. You might grow shade lovers in the shadows of sun worshippers or place companion plants close to one another to make your space as sustainable as possible.

Convenience

You'll be more likely to succeed if you pay attention to the things that will make taking care of crops quick and easy. So, in addition to keeping frequently used plants close at hand, make sure tools, compost and a water supply are easily accessible. If it's a lot of hassle to rig up a hosepipe you might not bother. If, on the other hand, you have a couple of water butts nearby with a hosepipe permanently attached, watering will become a pleasure not a chore.

Storage

Have you thought about storage in your small garden? You'll need somewhere safe and dry for bags of compost, seeds, a watering can or hosepipe, some hand tools such as a fork and trowel and spare containers or potting compost. Work all of this into your plan now – will you need a small storage container, can you utilize an existing shed or do you need to find somewhere in the house for these items?

You may not be lucky enough to have a shed but you will need to find somewhere to store your materials.

Putting it all Together

Now you've learned about space, sunlight and compost, how can you piece everything together to design a functional and beautiful container garden? Here's a quick recap:

 Have you utilized south-facing walls to their fullest?

 Do you have partial shade that you need to plan for?

 Could you use reflective materials to maximize light?

 Ensure you leave plenty of space between containers for you to water, weed and harvest.

 Ensure you have plenty of sturdy supports for climbing plants.

 Are your containers robust enough to withstand high winds in exposed areas?

 Keep tender plants and your favourites closest to your house.

 Keep tools, compost and a supply of water handy – convenience equals success!

Did You Know?

The best place to store seeds is in the fridge.

Checklist

Before you get started on your pots, keep in mind the following:

Budget: Do you have a budget in mind for gardening? You'll need to take into account tools, seeds, containers, fertilizer and compost.

Space: How much space do you have to grow? Enough room for a couple of hanging baskets or ground space for containers and growbags?

Extra space: Is there any way you could extend your growing space; perhaps by using window boxes, growing on indoor sills or putting up hanging baskets?

Light: What are the light conditions of your plot? Are there some areas that get at least eight hours of sunlight each day? If you don't get much sunlight, you'll need to limit yourself to more shade-tolerant crops or grow indoors on a sunny windowsill.

Compost: Do you make your own compost or will you have to buy some? Compost can be quite expensive, so add this to your budget. Is there room for a small compost heap on your plot? You could even make a wormery if your space is very limited.

Layout: How can you make the most of your small space? By grouping taller plants at the back you can leave room for smaller crops such as herbs towards the front. Will you need to move pots around? If so, consider getting planters on wheels to make this easier.

What
to Grow

Selecting Crops

Now it's time to plan what you will grow! You've spent time learning about the benefits of growing your own food and you've been assessing your own plot to check space and light conditions. Now it's time to choose what to grow. Before you rush out and buy packets of seeds, it's worth remembering a few things.

Taking Stock

It's very tempting to buy lots of exotic sounding seeds, determined to grow something unusual or grow lots of different types of crops. Before you do that, think about a few things such as

what you actually *like* to eat, how much space you have and your time, energy and budget. It would be disheartening if your first growing season was a failure due to poor planning.

Taste

There is little point wasting time and money on growing foods you don't like! Of course there are benefits to be gained from growing plants and tending them, but the main point of growing food is to enjoy eating it! Think about this when you are browsing seed catalogues, looking online or searching the shelves of your local garden centre.

Meal Planning

What fresh items do you buy every week when you shop? This will give you some clues about what you should grow. Most people are creatures of habit and the same items will creep into your kitchen cupboards week after week. There will be staple foods too that make the basis of all your meals. For some it's favourite vegetables, while others eat salad with every meal.

Family Food

What does your family like to eat? Do they eat the same as you or have different preferences? Gardening might be the perfect way to get a reluctant partner or child to try new foods! Think about your children's lunch boxes – are there items such as cherry tomatoes or carrots that you could grow? Do you or your partner have salad in your sandwiches or do most of your evening meals start with a base of onions and tomatoes?

Tasty Options

By taking a look at what you and your family eat in a typical week, you'll start to get ideas about what you would like to grow:

- **What are your favourite fresh foods?**
- **What fresh items do you buy every week?**
- **What staple foods make the basis of your weekly meals?**
- **Could growing fresh foods be a way to incorporate more healthy meals into your repertoire?**

Dietary Needs

Do you or your family have any special dietary needs? Perhaps you're all trying to get healthier – in which case growing your own fruit and vegetables is a great way to start. Maybe you are on a diet, in which case eating more fresh fruit and vegetables instead of convenience foods is a way to improve your chances of losing weight. Perhaps a change of circumstances has affected your finances in which case growing your own food is one way to stretch your budget.

From Pregnancy to Weaning

Each person has their own individual food requirements. Expectant mothers need a wide range of vitamins and minerals to stay healthy throughout pregnancy – what could be better than growing your own food and eating it fresh from the plant! In addition, container gardening provides you with gentle exercise and you don't need to do any heavy lifting or digging which can be a problem in traditional plots. You can later wean your baby on home-grown fruit and vegetable purées.

Toddlers and Young Children

Toddlers and young children can eat like a horse one day and a sparrow the next. All of this is perfectly normal but can make meal planning a nightmare. It can also lead to considerable food waste. By growing your own food, little fingers can help themselves to cherry tomatoes, salad leaves or carrot sticks as and when they want them. It's also easy to whip up a bowl of vegetable soup or a smoothie if the ingredients are on hand.

Teenagers

Teenagers can be just as fussy as toddlers! Encouraging them to help in the garden; even if they don't take an active interest, it's easy to incorporate good food into a teenage diet if it's right outside the door. Why not keep chopped vegetables ready prepared in the fridge with a selection of dips or batch-cook and freeze healthy meals so your teens can warm them through as a 'convenience' meal?

Busy Lives

If you're a busy executive, a full-time carer or juggling career and home it's even more important that you eat well. Meal preparation however, can go out of the window after a busy day at work. By growing your own food you'll have access to fresh, seasonal food which you can grab as easily as a takeaway. It's easy to add a few berries to your breakfast, eat salad with your meal or add health-giving herbs to your meals if they're outside your window.

Health Issues

Small, healthy meals are the key to maintaining health for elderly people or after illness. You can grow all the ingredients for hearty soups, healthy stir fries and many herbs have incredible health properties. For example, thyme can support the immune system, mint is excellent for digestive problems and sage makes an effective gargle for sore throats.

Did You Know?

The most widely used vegetable across the world is the onion.

Gardening for Your Needs

When deciding what to grow, it's important to take the needs of you and your family into account. Each person has individual dietary requirements and it's worth thinking about these before buying your first packet of seeds. Remember:

 Pregnant women: Expectant mothers need lots of vitamins and minerals; check which foods are highest in these important nutrients and consider growing some of them.

 Babies: Shop-bought baby food can be expensive. By growing your own food and puréeing it, you can make your own.

 Toddlers: You'll be less likely to have a 'faddy eater' if your toddlers are brought up around food – let them pick cherry tomatoes or take care of their own containers.

 Teenagers: Encourage teenagers to eat healthily by growing some vegetables and incorporating them into their favourite meals.

 Busy people: If you have a busy lifestyle, then good nutrition is paramount. Eating home-grown, seasonal and fresh produce is one way to achieve and maintain good health.

 Elderly and vulnerable: Growing ingredients for healthy soups, stews and casseroles can be ideal for the elderly or those who are convalescing.

Did You Know?

Several foods that we call vegetables are in fact fruits such as tomatoes, aubergines and peppers.

Space and Conditions

You've already learned a lot about accessing the space you have available and it's important to bear all this in mind when you're deciding what to grow. However, there are crafty ways to increase your growing space. For example growing vertically instead of concentrating on ground space is one way to increase your yield. This works especially well on patios or small courtyards. Don't forget about the other conditions of your plot too.

Maximizing Space

Using Shade

Some plants do not like too much sun or the heat of summer sun. In this case growing them in the shade of climbing sun lovers is another way to increase your yield in a small space. This is how the principles of permaculture work; letting nature support itself. In a natural environment shade lovers grow in the shade of sun lovers. Plants that need support grow around other plants. Plants that don't compete for nutrients and water grow together in harmony.

Window Boxes

If you're limited to very small containers such as window boxes you won't be able to grow a row of large cabbages, but you can successfully grow lettuces and some herbs. Most people waste half the salad they buy because it goes off before they can eat it all, so don't underestimate the power of being self-sufficient in salad leaves! Shop-bought herbs often die soon after you get them home – you'll have much more success with home grown, so these make ideal plants for window boxes.

Hanging Baskets

Maybe you don't have outdoor ledges or a balcony but you have a free south-facing wall. In this case hanging baskets or wall planters are for you! Even though they are small and require vigilant watering, some crops can thrive if well looked after. There are special varieties of tumbling cherry tomatoes that grow well in hanging baskets. Strawberries, edible plants such as nasturtiums and even some herbs can be a success. With planning and care you could grow an entire meal in a few hanging baskets!

Space for Your Plants

Some plants such as squash like to spread themselves sideways, whereas beans can grow very tall. All of this needs to be taken into account when deciding what to grow. Do you have room to let plants spread or do you need more compact crops such as carrots? If you are growing on a roof garden or balcony will high winds be a problem to tall crops? The last thing you want is your crop being damaged by a strong gust of wind. If you don't have enough room to allow your plants to spread, they will not reach their full potential.

Space for You

Don't forget that you need space too! Although it's tempting to fill the plot with all sorts of containers and crops you need room to manoeuvre safely and easily. If it's difficult to get around your containers to tend to your plants, the chances are you'll have some casualties to deal with. Allow room around the containers for you so that watering, tending and harvesting is easy and pleasurable.

Space Requirements Recap

You'll now be familiar with your gardening plot. How much space do you have and how much can you dedicate to container gardening? Some helpful tips:

- **Space**: Have you worked out how much space you can dedicate to container gardening?
- **Growing upwards**: If ground space is limited, could you grow vertically to increase your yield?
- **Permaculture**: Could you incorporate the principles of permaculture to make your site more productive?
- **Window boxes**: What could you grow in window boxes outside your kitchen window? Herbs or salads are a good idea.
- **Hanging baskets**: Don't forget hanging baskets too – tumbling tomatoes or strawberries work well in these.
- **Space to garden**: Remember to leave room for yourself to move around your containers!

Top Tip

Try and eat five portions of fruit and vegetables a day as part of a healthy diet.

Conditions

Not all gardening plots are created equal! While some may have the perfect south-facing patio or decking, others will be struggling with limited light and less-than-optimum settings. With a bit of forethought most situations, apart from a tiny north-facing space, can be overcome.

Sunlight

If sunlight is restricted you'll either need to grow crops that can tolerate partial shade, use reflective surfaces to increase light or remove structures that are casting shadows. Alternatively, you may have to abandon your container garden site and find somewhere else. This could mean using window boxes on the other side of your home, utilizing hanging baskets or using a sunny window sill inside your home.

Prevailing Winds

If your container garden is going to be on a balcony or roof garden, or if you live in a particularly exposed area, then prevailing winds can be a problem. Tall container crops are particularly prone to damage from wind. If you live in a windy area, look for compact 'bush' varieties of plants and steer clear of crops that grow very tall such as runner beans. You may need to build some form of wind break if conditions are very harsh or move pots inside during winter.

If you want to grow peas on a windy roof garden, make sure you choose low-growing bush varieties.

Drought

Plants grown in containers will dry out more quickly than those planted in the ground and they will rely on you for daily watering. If you live in a dry climate this is especially important. In this instance you might have to plan for drought-resistant varieties and forego plants that need a lot of water or you may need to budget for an irrigation system to make watering easier.

Conditions Recap

If you have limited sunlight or live in a very exposed site you'll need to plan your crops as these are not the best conditions for container plants to thrive. Think about the following:

- **Sunlight**: Is sunlight restricted in your area? Think about reflective surfaces, look for obscuring structures or rethink your plot completely.
- **Wind**: If prevailing winds are an issue, you'll need to plant low-level crops such as compact 'bush' varieties. You may also need to offer support to plants and install windbreaks.
- **Rain**: In areas with low rainfall you'll have to be vigilant about watering.
- **Water**: If lack of water is an issue, plan for drought-resistant crops or install an irrigation system.

Top Tip

Be careful when using dark-coloured containers because they absorb heat which could possibly damage the plant roots.

Time and Energy

Gardening requires time and patience, but can be planned and designed around your other commitments. A small established container garden might only take you a couple of hours a week to maintain, but there will be times such as the sowing and harvesting season that require more work and you'll have to schedule this into your arrangements.

Saving Time

Short Cuts

You can, of course, forgo the sowing altogether and buy established plants from a nursery or garden centre for transplanting into your prepared containers. This cuts out all the time needed for sowing seeds, transplanting seedlings and taking care of them. It can be a great way for novice gardeners to see which crops are easy to take care of and which provide the best harvest.

You may want to take a short cut and visit the garden centre to buy some established plants to get you started.

Share the Work

Are there members of your family or some friends who could help out in the garden? Gardening is a great family activity where you all work together to achieve a common goal. And there's no better goal than enjoying delicious home-grown food! You could set up a rota and ask your family to join in; you'll all be getting fresh air, learning some new skills and getting gentle exercise too.

Scheduling

Are there windows of opportunity in your weekly schedule that you could dedicate to gardening? Most of us say we 'have no time' but the reality is we prioritize it for other things; the most common one being the television. Is there a programme you just can't miss? Perhaps you could record it and reward yourself at the weekend or late one evening for all your hard work in the garden by sitting down and watching it. Maybe you need to let another commitment go; this might be the perfect time to ditch the committee you are on and have been feeling fed up with for some time!

Making Time

Whether or not we can find time to do things is really about what we *choose* to do. We all have choices and it might be that you need to stop one activity in order to pursue your gardening.

Perhaps you are a 'yes' person and beginning your own container garden would be the perfect way to learn to say 'no'. Maybe you could give up the gym and make your garden your outdoor gym. By the time you've shifted a few pots around, carried compost and stretched around plants to weed you'll be fit and healthy.

Top Tip

TimeBanks are groups of people who swap skills with one another – perfect for gardening!

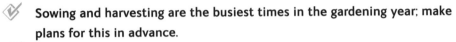

Careful Planning

Time is probably the one thing we wish we all had more of, but it's possible to create time by taking an honest look at our weekly schedule:

- ✅ **Sowing and harvesting are the busiest times in the gardening year; make plans for this in advance.**
- ✅ **Successive sowing is a way to make your time commitment work for you.**
- ✅ **Buying established plants means you don't have a busy sowing season.**
- ✅ **Work out a rota with family or friends and enlist their help.**
- ✅ **Could you forego a TV programme or give up some other commitment?**
- ✅ **Could your garden become your 'green gym' – you'll save money too!**

Energy

As well as time you need energy to dedicate to gardening. Once your seedlings are established they need lots of tender, loving care. This is especially true of crops grown in pots. Container crops are more reliant on you for water and the correct nutrition, and once you move into summer, and the temperature increases and rainfall decreases, you'll need even more energy to keep up!

Energy Levels

How much energy do you have? Are you a young person with boundless energy and enthusiasm or a busy working mum who is juggling every last drop of energy into a busy schedule? Perhaps you're a career man with a small amount of energy at the end of your day or you are limited by physical ability. There will be a way to make container gardening work for you, but you may need to compromise on your original plan.

Energy Boost

If you have unlimited energy then gardening is a great way to use some up! You'll find you sleep better if you can get outdoors each day and you can make container gardening as easy or challenging as you wish. You can create your growing area by making your own containers and supporting structures and by the time you've moved around a few bags of compost you'll be putting your excess energy somewhere useful and productive.

Juggling

Your schedule may already be busy, so adding another project to your week will be the last thing you feel like doing, but gardening may be just the thing. If you're a busy person juggling work, home life and other commitments it's important to get some 'me time'. Tending to a few containers and harvesting your own food is a great way to enjoy some solitude. Many people feel their employers and even their own families take them for granted, so taking care of plants is a great way to feel good about yourself.

Get Help

Don't be afraid to ask for help. You could turn your small container garden into a community project. Younger members of your family might be eager to get their hands in the soil. Friends might pop over a couple of times a week to help out in exchange for food later in the year. Join a TimeBank and see if members in your area are able to give you a couple of hours a week of their time or barter with a friend – an hour of babysitting for an hour of gardening.

Did You Know?

Permaculture uses patterns that occur in nature to maximize effect, minimize work and bring about sustainable land use.

Make it Easy

If you are limited due to physical ability there are plenty of ways to make container gardening simple to maintain. If bending or kneeling is a problem, containers can be matched to the height you need them. You can support them on bricks or pallets, which is advisable anyway to allow air to circulate around each pot or you could use raised beds. You could grow food on indoor window sills which are easily reached or try herbs on the kitchen work surface.

Energy Patterns

Everybody has their own unique energy pattern. Some have more than others and seem to run from one thing to another. Others have limited energy and another project might feel like a chore. Here are some ways to run a successful container garden despite limited energy:

- 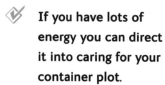 **If you have lots of energy you can direct it into caring for your container plot.**
- **Utilize your energy by going for the DIY approach – make your own containers, supporting structures and compost.**
- **Instead of viewing gardening as 'another chore' see it as some valuable 'me time' where you can be alone, lost in thought.**
- **Enlist the help of family members, friends or neighbours.**
- **Make your garden work for you – if you have physical limitations, design your garden around your needs.**
- **Consider indoor gardening if you feel unable to manage an outdoor space.**

Money Matters

It's true you'll need a certain amount of money to set up your container garden. How much you need depends solely on your plans and goals. If money is no object then buying assorted containers, bags of compost and tools won't be a problem, but if your budget is limited you will need to make every penny count.

Cheaper Option

Are there some foods you don't buy because they are too expensive? While root crops are relatively cheap, foods like tomatoes and peppers can cost more. Perhaps these would be the perfect excuse to grow your own. Next time you're shopping compare prices of fresh foods and see which ones are out of your price range. Next take a look at how easy it might be to grow these foods and add these to your list of foods you'd like to grow.

Cutting Costs

Gardening can be very expensive, but the growing trend towards the 'make do and mend' approach can save lots of money as well as being better for the environment. Our convenient lifestyle often comes at a price. Yes it's more convenient to write a long list of everything you want and head to a garden centre to buy the lot, but with some planning and searching around, you might be able to get lots of things much cheaper or even for free.

Top Tip

If you want to grow more than one crop in a container, select plants that will be happy with the same amounts of water, sun, heat and food.

Recycling

Maybe you have things lying around at home already that would be perfect – anything can be used for a gardening container as long as it has drainage holes and is big enough. Old saucepans with broken handles, a bucket with a hole in it, even spare car tyres can be used to grow food. If you scour your sheds and garages you might find items that can double up as tools. You'll find an entire chapter dedicated to this later in the book.

Make a Wish-list

If you're serious about gardening but don't have the funds to set it up then why not put items onto a wish-list? When your birthday comes around you could ask for gardening items or gift vouchers. Alternatively put aside some money every month for your gardening fund. With careful purchasing you'll be amazed how far your money can go. Another idea is to get a temporary part-time job. Choose something that you enjoy and can be fitted around other commitments so it doesn't become a chore or give something up such as your daily latte and put the money into a savings fund.

Find the Money

Don't let a limited budget stop you growing your own food. There are plenty of ways to fund your project and, let's face it, we always manage to find money for the things we *really* want to do, from enjoying a drink at the end of the week to spending money on a haircut. It's all a question of prioritizing.

 It's worth shopping around several garden centres and even browsing online to see if you can get better value for money.

 You'll find an array of gardening equipment in household stores or even pound shops. Check out charity shops and thrift stores too.

 Make a note of expensive food in shops and see if you could grow it yourself.

 Take a look around your home and see what you could use for containers.

 Create a wish-list and send it to people before your birthday.

 Get a part-time job to fund your gardening project.

 Give something up and put aside the money for containers, tools, seeds and compost.

Checklist

Before you decide what to grow, consider the following:

- **Taste**: What do you and your family actually *like*? There is little point planting things nobody wants to eat!

- **Staples**: What meals do you eat every week? This should give you a clue about some staple foods you could consider eating.

- **Diet**: What dietary needs does your family have? Pregnant mums, weaning babies and toddlers have different needs to teenagers or the elderly.

- **Space**: Have you had a good look at the space available to you? Do you need to think outside the box and grow vertically or utilize hanging baskets and wall planters?

- **Time**: How much time can you commit to your container garden – can you enlist help in any way or will you need to 'create' time by giving something up?

- **Adaptability**: How can you make your garden work for you? Raising containers so you can sit at them and installing irrigation systems are some ideas to make gardening easier.

Preparing to Grow

Gathering Supplies

Not long to go before you can get stuck into your gardening experience! So far you've learned about the benefits of growing your own food in containers, how to determine the best layout and design for your lifestyle and situation and how to choose what to grow. Now you need to source the basics – seeds, compost, fertilizers, tools and suitable containers.

Sourcing Your Supplies

The best place in which to gather your items is your local garden centre. You can get expert advice and find a large variety of items on offer. You'll also be able to take advantage of loyalty schemes, free gardening catalogues or end of season sales. You can buy things online, but until you know what you are looking for, it's better to go into a shop where you can see the quality of items and try out tools.

Seeds

You can buy vegetable seeds at your garden centre but you can also get virtually any type of seed via the internet. You can also take part in seed swaps and even pick up seeds in some supermarkets along with your weekly shopping. A lovely way to spend a winter evening is flicking through seed catalogues and imagining your garden in the springtime.

Compost

Compost can be bought from garden centres, online and from some general household stores or gathered from a willing friend. The best sort of compost, however, is made at home! If you have the space, consider setting up a compost area. You can buy compost bins especially for small spaces; they don't take up much room but allow you to turn your dead plants and kitchen scraps into a valuable resource.

Fertilizers

Fertilizers are probably best bought from a garden centre, as you can get expert advice on the right ones for your needs. Choosing fertilizers can be bewildering at first, so talk to someone who can give you the best advice. Once you know what you need, these can be bought from some local stores or online, or you can even make your own organic fertilizers!

All sorts of things can go into making your own compost. Note that eggshells should be crushed, and only the contents of polyester tea bags added.

Tools

All you really need for container gardening is a hand trowel, hand fork, gardening gloves, a watering can or hosepipe and secateurs if you are growing fruit bushes. As you need so few tools this is one area where it's worth buying the best you can afford. It's the difference between getting the job done efficiently and tearing your hair out because the tool doesn't work effectively! Buy the best tools you can afford and spend time holding hand-held tools before buying to make sure they feel comfortable.

Containers

The next section goes into the wealth of options for your containers!

Pots, Glorious Pots

In this section you'll discover everything there is to know about garden containers. You can be forgiven for thinking your choices are limited to plastic or terracotta but, as you'll discover, there are many types of pots available, some of which you might already have at home! You can grow plants in virtually anything that holds soil and has holes in the bottom for drainage. Your only limit is your imagination and it's a great excuse for some creative recycling!

Plastic

Plastic pots are readily available, cheap to buy and a popular choice. They are lightweight, making them easy to move around and are perfect if you don't want to spend a lot of money on gardening. You can buy them in a variety of sizes and will find square, rectangular, round as well as other shapes. This means you can fit pots with straight sides into corners of your patio, balcony or roof garden.

Many Benefits

Plastic pots are strong and flexible despite their light weight. They are available in all sorts of colours to blend into the background or make a statement! Plastic pots are great for moisture-loving plants as they retain water well and do not wick it away like some materials. Plastic is an inert material suitable for growing edible plants.

Advantages of Plastic Pots

- ☑ **Cheap to buy and easy to find.**
- ☑ **Lightweight, strong and flexible.**
- ☑ **Lots of different sizes, shape and colours available.**
- ☑ **Good for gardeners who forget to water!**
- ☑ **Perfect for moisture-loving plants.**
- ☑ **Inert material means it is safe for food.**

Problems with Plastic

Plastic pots have their downfalls too. Despite being cheap they are not very environmentally friendly unless made from recycled plastic. Once they are no longer wanted they are difficult to recycle in some areas so can end up in landfill. As the plastic is quite thin, these containers offer little by way of insulation which means summer sun can heat up the contents to damaging levels. During the winter, temperature drops can destroy plants.

UV Damage and Over Watering

Plastic is prone to UV damage and can become brittle or discoloured very quickly. Dark-coloured pots such as black or dark green can absorb so much heat from the sun in the height of summer that the soil heats up and destroys the plant roots. Even though they are better for gardeners who forget to water occasionally, they can keep soil too wet when over watered which leads to rotting roots.

Disadvantages of Plastic Pots

- Made from non-renewable resources.
- Difficult to recycle in some areas.
- Offer little insulation to soil and plants.
- Can suffer from UV damage and become brittle.
- Can fade and become unsightly.
- Easy to waterlog plants and rot the roots.

Did You Know?

Most plastic pots are made from polypropylene or polystyrene which makes them hard to recycle in some countries.

Plastic: PVC

Many window boxes are now made from PVC, which makes them very stable. Due to their popularity, prices are coming down all the time, making PVC one of the cheaper options.

Advantages of PVC

- Rot and moisture free.
- Unattractive to insects.
- Does not crack or warp.
- Can be painted to look like wood.
- A cheaper choice.

Disadvantages of PVC

Along with the numerous advantages of PVC, there are some disadvantages too. PVC is made from non-renewable resources and is difficult to recycle, so it's not the ideal material for end disposal.

- PVC is made from non-renewable resources.
- PVC is difficult to recycle.
- Insulation is not good, so soil can get too hot in summer or too cold in winter.

Fibreglass boxes can be made to have a stone or terracotta effect.

Plastic: Fibreglass

Fibreglass (glass-reinforced plastic) is also a good option and ideal for use both inside and out. They can be painted or can be bought in a style that looks like stone. Fibreglass boxes will last a lifetime.

Advantages of Fibreglass

There are several advantages to fibreglass including:

- **Less expensive than stone.**
- **Low maintenance.**
- **Lightweight.**
- **Frost proof and non-corrosive.**
- **Lasts a long time.**

Disadvantages of Fibreglass

Although it has many good points, fibreglass is a brittle material, so if it is knocked or dropped it can chip or even crack. It is also a very thin material with poor insulation properties. This is fine if your climate is fairly stable throughout the year, but if you experience very hot summers or harsh winters it might not be the best material to use. As fibreglass is so hard wearing, it is also expensive.

 Brittle – may crack or chip if dropped.
 Poor insulation – compost can freeze in winter and overheat in summer.
 Expensive as it is so hard wearing.

Terracotta

Terracotta pots are readily available in garden centres and are very popular. The material is durable and attractive. They are quite heavy which makes them ideal for exposed areas; there is no risk of them blowing over in the wind, even with tall crops in them. You can buy terracotta containers in many different shapes and sizes to fit into your space.

Many Benefits

Terracotta pots are sturdy and if looked after can last many years. Unglazed pots are available in the traditional terracotta colour but you can buy glazed ones in all colours of the rainbow. Terracotta pots wick away moisture from the plants which means risk of over watering is reduced. Terracotta is easily recycled after use and is safe for growing food crops.

Advantages of Terracotta Pots

- ✅ Readily available in garden centres.
- ✅ Sturdy and long lasting.
- ✅ Lots of different sizes, shape and colours available.
- ✅ Good for gardeners who tend to over water.
- ✅ Easily recycled after use.
- ✅ Inert material means it is safe for food.

Problems with Terracotta

The most obvious downside to terracotta pots is that they break easily if dropped or knocked. Some cheaper pots crack in the frost because water gets into the material, freezes and expands. Glazed pots can stop this happening. Terracotta pots can take much needed moisture from some plants and so require more watering, but this is not an issue with glazed pots.

Water and Cost

If you're the sort of gardener who leaves plants to wilt before watering, clay pots are not the best choice. Clay pots can remove too much moisture from seedlings so it might be better to transplant into plastic pots if you're worried about keeping the soil moist enough. Terracotta pots have the habit of forming a white layer on the outside from water deposits that some gardeners find unsightly. In addition, clay pots are much more expensive than plastic ones.

Disadvantages of Terracotta Pots

- Terracotta pots break easily.
- Cheaper pots can crack in the frost.
- Can remove too much water for gardeners who tend to under water.
- Can look unsightly when white deposits form on the outside.
- Much more expensive than plastic pots.

Biodegradable Pots

Other pots that are great for the environment are biodegradable pots. These can be made from coir, wood fibre, latex, rice husk, recycled paper, textile fibres or cardboard. The beauty of these is there is no landfill waste. They are surprisingly hard wearing; while some are designed for seedlings, planted into the ground and then rot away, other biodegradable pots last for up to two seasons.

Top Tip

If you're overrun with pots, why not offer them to a local allotment owner instead of throwing them away?

How Coir Pots are Made

Coir fibres are separated from the coconut husks and tossed in a 'drum' to separate the coir granules from the fibres. The fibres are then washed in fresh water, dried in the sun and formed into pot shapes. When the pots are dry, they are dipped in latex and then trimmed, inspected and packed.

Biodegradable Pros

The main advantage to using biodegradable pots is environmental. Whereas plastic is made from oil, a non-renewable resource (which needs refining, and chemicals to produce the pots) biodegradable pots are made from constantly renewed, natural resources. As many are plant based this has the added bonus of the plants themselves reducing CO_2 emissions. Finally, these pots biodegrade, so the natural resource returns to the soil – just as nature intended!

Other benefits include:

- Semi-rigid and surprisingly strong.
- Lightweight and will not break when dropped.
- Keep roots moist and warm.
- Made from renewable sources and do not contribute to landfill.

Biodegradable Cons

The disadvantages to using biodegradable pots
are mainly associated with cost and availability.
It's much quicker and easier to source plastic or
terracotta containers and you need to remember
to replace biodegradable pots, so there is an
ongoing cost.

Other drawbacks include:

 More expensive than plastic pots.

 Availability can be limited.

 **Need to remember to have more pots
in stock for when these biodegrade.**

 **Not all pots are made equal; some
use glues so are not biodegradable
at all.**

Reusing Containers

Finding suitable containers to grow food in doesn't have to cost anything at all. If you take a
look around your home, shed, garage, basement or attic you'll find all sorts of things that are
perfect. As long as the container is deep enough and big enough you can grow many different
crops from small clumps of chives to potatoes.

Did You Know?

**The UK uses over 5 million tonnes of plastic each year of which an estimated
19 per cent is currently being recovered or recycled.**

Raised Beds

Raised beds are ideal if you have a decent-sized patio to build them on. You can buy pre-made beds which you slot together or you can make your own from a variety of materials. Raised-bed gardening is very popular, even for people who have large gardens as there are several advantages to them over an open plot e.g. you can control the environment of the raised bed, weeding is much easier and you can extend the growing season.

Using Raised Beds

Raised beds are basically large boxes of compost. They are usually 1–1.2 m (3–4 ft) wide and any length to suit the size of your plot. You can make them anything from 30 cm (12 in) deep to waist high, which is perfect for people who find it hard to bend or kneel. Raised beds lend themselves to permaculture principles because you tend to pack plants in more densely to create a micro-climate where moisture is conserved and weeds are suppressed by plant growth.

Materials

Raised beds are usually made from wood. You need to choose the source carefully and ensure it hasn't been treated with anything that could leach into the soil and contaminate your food. Other materials are concrete blocks, which are cheaper but not as nice to look at, or polyurethane.

Advantages of Raised Beds

Raised-bed gardening is a popular choice for many reasons. Some of the benefits of using raised beds are:

- Ability to control the soil quality.
- Crops are planted closer together resulting in natural weed suppression and moisture control.
- Can be built to any height, making them ideal for people with physical limitations.
- Ideal if you want to try permaculture or square foot gardening.

More about Raised Beds

Raised beds can be one of the more expensive options. The containers are quite large and by the time you've bought compost to fill them (and don't forget it will need to be replenished every two or three years) the ongoing cost can be significant. Raised beds are heavy, so not suitable for some plots such as balconies.

Disadvantages of Raised Beds

Raised beds have some drawbacks, as follows:

- Can be expensive to buy if you're not able to make your own.
- Filling with compost can be costly as they're usually quite big.
- Impossible to move once filled.
- Not suitable where weight limit is an issue e.g. balcony or roof garden.

Window Boxes

Window boxes are rectangular containers usually supported by brackets and situated outside your windows. They are traditionally used for flowers, but can be used for herbs and other edible plants. Window boxes are usually made out of wood or plastic, but you can buy them in fibreglass and metal as well as other materials. They range from rustic looking to ornate and fancy ironwork. Window boxes are the containers that come in the biggest variety of materials.

Using Window Boxes

Window boxes are ideal for people who live in high-rise housing or have little or no outside land. They are usually around 15-20 cm (6-8 in) deep so are only suitable for certain plants. As they are outside windows you would not grow tall plants in them otherwise this would obscure your view and the plant would be unsteady with such little depth to the container.

Maintaining Window Boxes

Window boxes are maintained by opening the window and reaching out! Just be aware of people walking underneath when you tend or water your boxes. They are ideal for putting

Top Tip

To make window-box gardening more economical, you can find instructions online for making your own containers.

outside your kitchen window, especially for herbs or salads where you can lean out and snip the leaves from whatever plant you want to eat. They can also be used indoors if you have deep enough windowsills.

Self-watering Option

Self-watering window boxes can help if you are a gardening novice or you are often away from home. Automatic watering systems allow you to go up to three months without worrying about keeping the soil in your plants moist! These are particularly helpful indoors when the temperature can fluctuate at different times of the year.

Wrought Iron

Wrought iron, which is mainly used for window boxes, offers distinctive styling. Often called 'window baskets' or 'hayracks', these types of baskets are lined with coir (coconut husks) to retain your plants and soil. The quality of the finish will determine how long the ironwork remains looking good.

Advantages of Wrought Iron

 Strong and long-lasting.
 Elegant design.

Disadvantages of Wrought Iron

The main disadvantage is that it will eventually rust. While this might look 'antique' for a while it will gradually erode and deteriorate, which could make it unsafe. Wrought iron is heavy and requires strong fixings to your home.

 Heavy material.
 Usually only available in black.
 Once it rusts it slowly deteriorates.

Aluminium

Aluminium is very low maintenance. It is rust proof, lightweight and strong and can be styled to look like wrought iron – so a safer alternative for window boxes. You can buy them in recycled materials to make less impact on the environment.

Advantages of Aluminium

 Low maintenance.

 Rust proof.

 Can be bought in recycled materials and recycled after use.

 **Lightweight.**

Disadvantages of Aluminium

Aluminium is soft, so can scratch easily which means even when fairly new, it can look worn. The colour can dull quickly too. You might buy a shiny silver surface, only to be looking at dull grey in a few months' time! It also has poor insulation which isn't good for plants.

 Scratches easily, so can look shabby quite quickly.

 Silver colour can soon turn a dull grey.

 Poor insulation can freeze or fry plants!

Wood

Wood is a popular choice for containers – especially for window boxes. You can stain, paint or leave it natural; it is affordable – in fact it's usually the cheapest option; and it is a natural, renewable material – look for containers made from wood sourced from well-managed forests. At the end of their use, wooden window boxes will compost, making them a good environmental choice.

Advantages of Wood

- Popular – easy to find and purchase.
- Can be stained, painted or left natural.
- Good economical choice – you can even make your own.
- Made from natural and renewable resource.

Disadvantages of Wood

Although it is a common choice, wood will deteriorate over time. It will gradually absorb moisture and wood-loving insects can do damage. In addition, environmental elements such as temperature fluctuations or driving rain can damage the wood. This means wooden containers require ongoing maintenance compared to other materials.

- Require regular maintenance.
- Will not last for ever.
- Can be damaged by adverse weather.
- Can be damaged by wood-boring insects.

Preparing Containers

Now you've planned the design of your container garden, chosen which types of containers to use and have ascertained which crops will grow best based on your confidence level, time commitments and financial circumstances, it's time to prepare your containers.

What You Need

You need the following items for setting up your container:

- ☑ Suitable base for the container.
- ☑ Your chosen container.
- ☑ Drainage material.
- ☑ Growing medium.
- ☑ Seeds or plants.
- ☑ Trowel or hand fork.

A Firm Base

If you are growing food in pots on a patio, balcony or rooftop your containers will need a suitable base to stand on. The base needs to be level, firm and able to withstand the weight of several full containers of soil. If you are going to use window boxes, hanging baskets or wall-mounted containers then this doesn't apply. People with a courtyard or small garden often have patio paving slabs, concrete or decking which are ideal.

Raising the Base

All containers need to be kept slightly above ground level to let air flow underneath and to prevent the plant and pot sitting in water. This is especially important for wooden containers that will rot if left in contact with water. Some stone troughs have built in 'legs' to achieve this. For other containers you'll need to buy or make your own. Old bricks or chunks of wood are ideal. Alternatively you can buy terracotta 'legs' which sit under the corners of your chosen container.

The Container

You've read all about the most popular types of containers for gardening. Whether you've chosen a terracotta pot, plastic planter or stone trough, you must make sure the container has drainage holes at the bottom. Most plants will die if their roots are kept in water for too long. The majority of containers have holes already in them, but you will have to make them yourself if they don't.

Drainage Material

As well as holes at the bottom of your container you will need a 5 cm (2 in) layer of suitable drainage material. Traditionally this would be stones or gravel, but if you want to save money or reuse items, old broken crocks or broken up polystyrene work well too. You may be able to get some broken crocks from a garden centre for free.

Top Tip

Using a flat trolley with wheels underneath your pots gives you much more manoeuvrability on your plot.

Growing Medium

Water your chosen growing medium so it is just damp. This helps it absorb water when you have your plants or seeds in it. Fill your container up to within 3 cm (1 in) of the rim. For most seeds and plants, potting or multi-purpose compost will be fine. For environmental reasons, it is better to avoid the use of peat-based composts. Once your pot is ready, you're ready to sow seeds or transplant seedlings!

Recap

In order to prepare your pot you need to:

 Ensure that your container has a firm base.

 Raise your container off the ground.

 Make sure your container has drainage holes in the base.

 Put a 5 cm (2 in) layer of drainage material in the bottom of the pot.

 Fill your container with growing medium such as multi-purpose compost.

The Gardening Year

To be prepared, it helps to be aware of when you'll be busy throughout the year. Weather varies around the world, but the basic gardening year remains the same wherever you are. Just like nature you'll have busy and restful periods too. The times between spring and autumn are the busiest where you'll be sowing, tending and harvesting. During the winter months your garden will be mainly dormant and that's a good time to do preparations and clearing ready for the next growing season.

Spring

Spring is a wonderful time of year. New shoots push their way through the soil and the first spring flowers or blossoms are always a joy to see. Spring can be one of the busiest times in your garden, especially if you haven't done all your maintenance and planning during the winter. During the spring you'll be sowing seeds indoors and out and you'll need to take control of any weeds before they take control of your containers.

Summer

During the summer your crops will be established and will need a lot of attention, particularly those in small containers. You'll need to establish regular watering and feeding patterns; keep on top of weeding and carry out successive sowing if you want a continual crop. You'll be able to harvest some herbs for use during winter and you'll need to be vigilant about pests and diseases.

Autumn

If you've had a successful growing season, autumn can be a busy time of harvesting. Although plants will be dying back there will still be lots for you to do. Regular picking can extend the growing season, dead plant growth will need to be removed and composted and you'll need to keep an eye on the weather. An early frost can kill plants, so you might need to protect or move more tender crops.

Winter

During the winter there is little to do in terms of care and feeding of plants. Most of the harvest will be over, but you might still be enjoying winter crops such as kale or some herbs. Winter is a great time to reflect on your year, work out what was successful or not, tidy up your plot and clean things ready for next year. You can look at seed catalogues, work out if there are any new supplies you need and hopefully be enjoying some of the preserved fruits of your labours!

Checklist

Before you start planting, it's wise to run through the following:

- **Cost**: What is your budget for pots?

- **Watering**: Do you tend to under or over water? This will influence the best materials for you.

- **Weight**: Will it be a problem to you if you cannot move the pots, such as heavy terracotta ones?

- **Wind**: Do you live in an exposed area where plastic pots could blow over?

- **Recycling**: Do you have anything at home that you could use as a pot?

- **Space**: Are you without ground space? If so you'll need to consider hanging baskets, wall planters and window boxes.

- **Raised beds**: Do you have space for raised beds? These can work exceptionally well for container gardening.

- **Seeds**: Start browsing seed catalogues and garden centres for the best seeds.

- **Compost**: Are you planning on making your own compost? Do you have a small compost bin or wormery set up?

- **Seasons**: Acquaint yourself with what you need to do when.

- **Drainage**: Do you have drainage materials at home such as broken crocks and polystyrene or will you need to buy gravel and stones?

How
to Grow

Sowing

Now the fun begins! After all the hard planning and design and after gathering your supplies you're ready to start! Most seeds are sown in spring when the weather warms up. Seeds need a certain consistent temperature to germinate although you can sow some seeds during autumn.

When and How to Sow

Although it's not rocket science, how, when and where you sow your seeds depends on the type of seeds, how many plants you want to end up with and what your growing conditions are.

For container gardening, you would sow your seeds in one of the following:

 Seed trays.

 Multi-cells.

 Individual pots.

 In situ (in the final container).

Seed Trays

Seed trays are readily available from garden centres. They are usually made from plastic and come in a range of sizes. They are cheap to buy and can be used again. They are literally a shallow tray that you fill with compost and sow your seeds into. Seed trays are ideal for growing large quantities of seeds, so might not be suitable if you only want a few of each

Top Tip

The best instructions for growing seeds are on the packets they come in! Be sure to read them thoroughly to find the best planting times.

plant. Some seed trays are large enough to be used as containers in their own right for short-rooted crops such as cut-and-come-again salad leaves and radishes.

Multi-cells

Multi-cell trays are very cheap to buy. They are made from thin plastic, which, unless you are very careful when pricking out, does tend to break after one season. With multi-cell trays you sow one seed per cell. This is a great way to see how much success you have had with germination.

Individual Pots

By using things you already have in your home such as old yogurt pots you can sow seeds individually. This is ideal if you only want two or three of a certain type of crop. It also means you don't need to transplant seedlings as you can move your plant straight from an individual pot to its final container. If you buy individual pots, they are readily available and cheap to buy. They can be reused year after year.

In Situ

Sowing seeds in situ saves you some work with transplanting, but you need to ensure the weather is warm and all risks of frost have passed for most seeds to germinate. Sowing in situ is ideal for larger plants such as runner beans and by using cloches you can increase chances of success. This saves on money needed for buying seed trays or small pots.

How to Sow Seeds

It doesn't matter what seeds you are sowing, you need the right compost. Find one that is very low in nutrients to avoid scorching the seedlings. Choose coir, which is a great peat substitute, a seed compost or mix 50 per cent multi-purpose and 50 per cent vermiculite. Sow the seed then cover with a thin layer of vermiculite or compost. Vermiculite protects the seed from moving around when you water it and helps prevent a 'crust' forming on top of the compost but doesn't stop light getting through. Label the containers with the types of seed and date.

Vermiculite can be used as part of your compost mix and as the final layer.

Top Tip

Store unused seeds in a plastic container at the bottom of your refrigerator.

Step by Step

Most seeds benefit from being sown in seed trays, multi-cells or individual pots before transplanting the mature plants. However you can sow direct into a large container. Whatever you choose, the method is virtually the same.

Step by step seed sowing for individual pots:

- **Gather your pots**: These can be bought specially or you can utilize things you have at home such as old yogurt pots.
- **Seedlings**: Make sure your seedling pots have adequate drainage otherwise seeds can rot.
- **Fill your pots**: Fill containers with compost and water carefully then leave the pots to drain.
- **Soaking pots**: Alternatively, stand pots in a large container of water to pull water up from the base for half an hour then drain.
- **Sewing seeds**: Carefully put two seeds into the pot (only use one seed for larger seeds such as runner beans).
- **Compost**: Sprinkle a fine layer of seed compost or vermiculite over the seeds (use the same depth of compost as the depth of the seed).
- **Cover up**: Cover the container with a plastic sheet or piece of glass (use a cloche if sowing in situ).
- **Germination**: When you see the first signs of germination take off the plastic and keep the compost moist.

Top Tip

You only need to cover the seed with compost – just a light sprinkling is fine.

Care of Seedlings

Once your seedlings emerge all you need to do is keep them warm and moist. Well almost! Once the seedlings come through, you can certainly breathe a sigh of relief, but they do have a few requirements to ensure they grow into healthy plants.

Space

If you've chosen to sow seeds in a seedling tray, you may need to thin them out when they come through. This means removing any weaker looking plants or removing ones that are growing too close to another. Seedlings do not like to be crowded because they need to get the right amount of water and nutrition. If they are too close they compete for nutrients and can all die.

Light

Seedlings naturally seek light and will grow towards it. They need as much light as possible which is why growing them in a windowsill is one of the best places. Two ways to increase the amount of light available are to select south-facing windowsills where available (but protect from strong, midday sun) or to put a piece of cardboard covered in aluminium foil as a 'wall' on the side of the container in the room – this helps reflect light back to the seedling.

Top Tip

Use a plant mister to 'water' seeds so you don't disturb the compost.

Moving On

If you notice roots coming out of the bottom of the pot it's time to move the seedlings into a bigger container. Keeping plants 'root bound' stunts their growth and can make them weak. Be aware that many plants do not like their roots disturbed, so you can minimize planting on by sowing them in individual pots. Then, instead of pricking out and planting on two or three times you can just move them into their final container.

Tender Loving Care

Caring for seedlings is pretty straightforward as long as you give them regular and frequent attention. Here's what you need to do:

- Ensure they are kept warm and the temperature does not fluctuate too much or too suddenly.
- Keep seedlings moist; without enough water they will die.
- Give seedlings light, but keep them away from strong direct sunlight which can scorch them.
- Do not allow the seedlings to become root bound as this can lead to stunted growth.

Transplanting

Congratulations! You've sown your seeds, they've emerged as seedlings and you've taken good care of them. Now they are ready for transplanting. Depending on the type of seed and size of pot this could be replanting into a slightly bigger pot or into their final container. If you can minimize the amount of times you plant on, so much the better. Minimal root disturbance leads to healthier and happier plants.

When to Transplant

The first two 'leaves' that appear on your seedlings are not leaves at all; they are part of the seed itself and provide stored food to the seedlings for a short period of time. On some plants it is very noticeable that they are different to the rest of the leaves. They usually have smooth edges and are a different shape to the 'true' leaves. If you have sown your seed in seedling trays, they are ready to 'prick out' and transplant when the plant has its first set of 'true' leaves.

How do I Know?

After around a week or two a seedling will produce its set of 'true' leaves and the first ones may shrivel and die. This is all perfectly normal, so no need to panic! The leaves that then appear will look more like an adult leaf. Timing is important with seedlings; if you put them out into the elements too quickly they may not survive. If you leave them too long they may become root bound.

The Pull Test

One week after the first set of true leaves have appeared, you should find your seedling has started to develop strong roots. You can test this by gently pulling on the seedling. It should hold itself firmly in the soil. If you have done any thinning out, you'll notice how easy it was to pull immature seedlings out of the compost. Once a plant can hold itself slightly and has its true leaves, it's ready for transplanting.

How to Transplant

Delicate seedlings require careful handling. Gently lift the seedling out of the soil using an old kitchen fork to help loosen the soil around the roots. You should always hold seedlings by their leaves and never by the stem. The stems are very thin and delicate and can snap easily. Place the seedling in a larger pot by filling it halfway with compost, adding the seedling and filling in with more compost. Water gently and put back in a light, warm place such as a windowsill.

Top Tip

Using biodegradable pots reduces root disturbances because you can plant the whole lot without taking the plant out of its pot.

Growing Up

As your seedlings grow into mature plants they will need more room, water and food. You'll eventually be moving them into their final growing containers, but this could take a series of steps as follows:

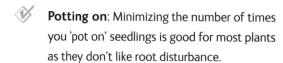

- ☑ **Potting on**: Minimizing the number of times you 'pot on' seedlings is good for most plants as they don't like root disturbance.
- ☑ **Bigger plants**: These get disturbed if you move them into too large a pot – follow instructions on seed packets.
- ☑ **In situ**: Some plants can be sown in situ e.g. runner beans.
- ☑ **Transplanting**: Wait until seedlings have their first set of 'true' leaves before pricking out and transplanting.
- ☑ **Lifting seedlings**: Lift small seedlings by their leaves, never by their stems as they can break easily.

Hardening Off

Once the roots have completely filled the second pot or the plants have three or four leaves, they're ready to be hardened off and planted outside. If you are growing your crops indoors, then you can skip this step. Hardening off is an important step as you don't want to shock your plants. Being grown indoors, plants do not experience much fluctuation in temperature; they've never felt wind or rain and have been pretty much protected from the elements.

How to Harden Off

Hardening off will prepare your plants for their final growing place and it's simple to do over the course of a week to 10 days. Ensure all risks of frost are passed, because once you have hardened off your plant it will be staying outdoors. On the first day move your plant outside for a few hours in a shaded area before bringing it back indoors. Repeat this process for a few days leaving the plant outside for a little longer each time.

Stepping it Up

Once your plant is happy outdoors for a full day, you can expose it to sunlight for a few hours. Continue to bring the plant back indoors at night-time and gradually build up the amount of time it spends during the day in the sunlight. When the plants are going out in the sun all day long you can safely transplant them outdoors into their final containers.

Moving Out

Once your plants are large enough it's time to move them to their final containers outside. If you keep a few things in mind, the hardening off process should be straightforward:

- **Moving outside**: Your plant is ready for the elements once they have three or four leaves or the roots are filling the pot.
- **Frost**: Ensure all risks of frost have passed before starting the hardening off process.
- **Timing**: The entire process can take seven to 10 days, so make sure you are around morning and afternoon to do this.
- **Adjusting**: Put your plant outside in a shaded area for a few hours and increase the number of hours over a few days.
- **Night-time**: Remember to bring the plants back indoors at night.
- **Sun**: When the plant is outside all day you can introduce it to a sunny site for a few hours a day and build this up too.
- **Transplanting**: When the plant is going out into the sun all day you can transplant them into their final growing containers outside.

Top Tip

A thin layer of vermiculite over seeds will help to protect them and prevent moisture loss.

Moving to Final Containers

Once your young plants have been hardened off you can transplant them into their final containers. Choosing a suitable day helps increase chances of survival and healthy growth. Don't opt for a bright sunny day or a windy rainy one. A calm, cloudy day is best. Young plants are as susceptible to hot midday sun as a ground frost, so pick a time when your plants can recover from the shock of being transplanted. Late afternoon is ideal.

Preparing to Transplant

Here's how to do it:

- **Drainage**: Make sure there are drainage holes and drainage materials in the base of your chosen container.
- **Compost**: Fill your container with suitable growing medium such as John Innes No. 2 and water it well. Leave it to drain so that it's nice and moist.
- **Making holes**: Use a trowel to make a small hole in the compost for your plant; ensure it is big enough to put the plant in with minimal disturbance.
- **Pricking out**: Hold your seedling pot upside down with the other hand cupped beneath it. Give the pot a gentle tap to allow the plant and root ball to come out.
- **Planting**: Pop the plants into the holes in the container you have prepared and make sure it's at the same level in the new pot as it was in the old pot.
- **Soil**: Firm the soil around the roots with your hands, being careful not to break the stem of the plant.
- **Water**: Give the plant a small drink of water and leave to recover!
- **Recovery**: Don't be shocked if your plants look almost dead a few hours after transplanting. They'll recover in a day or two.

Ongoing Care

Now your plants have reached their final growing place all you need to do is water, feed and weed them regularly to enjoy a good crop of produce at the end of the growing season. Each plant has slightly different requirements, but basic care is the same for all plants.

Watering

All plants require water in order to grow. However, it's not a case of the more the better. Too much water can drown plants or wash nutrients out of the soil.

Some plants tell you if they need watering because they start to wilt. For some crops this is fine, but for others, once they wilt they never recover. Likewise some plants can recover from over watering, but others don't. The best way to tell is to stick your finger down into the soil by about an inch. If the soil feels dry it needs watering.

Over watering

Surprisingly, more people over water plants than under water them. If your plants are looking in need of some tender loving care make sure the pot is draining correctly. Did you remember to check there were drainage holes and then put some draining materials such as gravel or broken crocks in the bottom? If not the water could be rotting the roots of your plants. If there are algae on the surface of the soil, this could be an indication of over watering.

Under watering

Some people under water their plants and this is a bigger risk with container gardening. Remember the plants are totally reliant on you for water, unlike plants that are in open ground. Under-watered plants can wilt and you might see some of the roots above the surface of the soil. Bottom leaves can turn yellow from either over OR under watering.

When to Water

Water is a precious resource that we should use responsibly and there are times of the day when any water you give to your plants will be best utilized. If you water in the midday sun all that happens is the water evaporates and doesn't go to the roots of your plants where it is needed.

Morning or Afternoon?

Early morning is the ideal time to water. It allows the water to reach the roots before the day gets too hot and the water evaporates. It also means the plant has water to use during the day as it gets hotter. If you go to work early then the next best time is early evening when the day is cooling down again. Don't water too late at night though; you need to leave time for the leaves to dry out otherwise they can get fungal diseases.

Automatic Watering

If you're really worried that you might not manage to successfully water your plants or you are away a lot during the summer, then automatic watering could be the answer. Irrigation systems vary from a fully controlled and timed system which can water 20 containers to a DIY version made from plastic bottles. You can buy watering spikes, water wicks and even self-watering containers.

Perfect Watering

Water is one of the most important things your plant needs. Get it wrong and you could have some casualties on your hands, but it's not hard to get it just right providing you remember the following:

- **Drainage**: Ensure your pots have adequate drainage material and holes before you plant your crops.
- **Watering**: Too much water can suffocate the roots of plants or wash nutrients away.
- **When to water**: If in doubt, stick your finger into the soil up to your first knuckle. If the soil feels dry, it needs watering.
- **Too much water**: Algae on the surface of your soil can mean you have over watered.

Too little water: If roots start to appear on the surface of the soil it can mean you have under watered.

 Timing: Water early morning for best results, or late afternoon if you're not around in the mornings.

 Automatic watering systems: These are a good idea if you are away a lot during the summer.

Top Tip

If you're worried about watering seedlings correctly, a self-watering container can help.

Feeding

Once your plants begin to grow fruit they will need feeding with fertilizers. Unlike crops grown in an open plot, your plants are more reliant on you for feeding and care. In a traditional plot, plants can take nutrients from the soil. In a container, the nutrients get used up quickly and need replacing. Fertilizers are concentrated forms of plant nutrients. They come in pellets, granules, powders or liquids and will improve plant growth and crop yields.

Why Use Fertilizer?

In a traditional plot with good quality soil you don't really need fertilizers. However, in containers where there is only a little soil, the plants will rely on you for nutritious meals so that you can enjoy yours later in the season! Some people report that using fertilizer gives them a better crop yield. In addition, fast-growing plants require more nutrients so will be healthier and stronger if you feed them. Fertilizers can be used when plants are showing signs of nutrient deficiency – this is often shown in leaf discolouration.

What's in Fertilizer?

The three major plant nutrients are Nitrogen (N), Phosphorus (P) and Potassium (K). These are needed to support healthy leaves, roots, flowers and fruits. They also help to keep the plant strong. Although there can be a bewildering array of fertilizers available, each one will state how much of each nutrient is in the product plus some brands will contain trace elements.

Inorganic and Organic

Inorganic fertilizers are made from synthetic components and deliver a more concentrated, faster-acting meal to your soil. Organic fertilizers are made from plant or animal ingredients such as seaweed, fish blood and bone or poultry manure and tend to be slower acting. You can make your own organic fertilizers from plants such as comfrey.

Comfrey can be used to make organic fertilizer.

Getting the Balance Right

Some fertilizers contain a mixture of nutrients in total balance or favour one nutrient more than others for the requirement of certain crops. Others provide just one nutrient and are used to correct a nutrient deficiency. Slow-release fertilizers are a mixture of nutrients that degrade slowly over time and are useful if you tend to forget to feed your crops or if you are away during the feeding season.

How Often?

Seeds need very low nutrient compost to germinate and if you feed the soil you might kill them. Once you have transplanted your plants into their final containers however, you can start feeding them with a multi-purpose fertilizer straight away. While they still have just leaves, feed them once every one or two weeks. When flowers start to appear you can increase this to once or twice a week. Once the fruit begins to set you can feed the plants every couple of weeks.

Top Tip

If you're concerned about getting things wrong, buy a fertilizer for the actual crop you are growing.

Different Plants Need Different Food

You'll discover that some plants need more of one nutrient than another and this can be reflected in particular fertilizers. For example one chilli and pepper fertilizer contains a 14:8:16 NPK ratio whereas a potato fertilizer contains NPK ratio of 3:5:7 and a root vegetable and onion fertilizer has an NPK ratio of 6:6:12 which favours high potassium to help plants become resistant to disease. It's worth taking your time to browse the available options and take the advice of an assistant in a garden centre.

Using Fertilizers

Although it can seem overwhelming at first, you'll soon get the hang of using fertilizers if you remember the following:

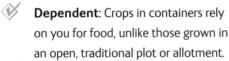

- **Dependent:** Crops in containers rely on you for food, unlike those grown in an open, traditional plot or allotment.
- **Nutrients:** The three major plant nutrients are Nitrogen (N), Phosphorus (P) and Potassium (K).
- **Inorganic fertilizers:** These are made from synthetic ingredients and are fast acting.
- **Organic fertilizers:** These are made from natural ingredients and take longer to work.
- **Nutrient mix:** Check each product for its NPK ratio to find the best one for your needs.
- **Do it yourself:** If you have access to comfrey or nettles, you can make your own fertilizers.
- **Directions:** Follow the directions on the product for how much to use and how often to use it.

Weeding

It is very important to keep weeds out of your containers. Once they grow roots they compete with your plants for water, nutrients and light. At their worst, weeds can strangle and suffocate plants. In addition, pests can hide underneath weeds and the weeds themselves can carry diseases. Fortunately weeding containers is straightforward as long as you adopt a 'little and often' approach. (*See* pages 167–68 for more on preventing and dealing with weeds.)

Tips for Weeding

Weeding can either be a huge chore or a satisfying job depending on how often and well you do it. Here are some tips to make weeding a pleasure:

- **Timing**: Create a weeding schedule. Work in short, sharp bursts throughout the week – this could be 10 minutes a day or two half hour slots a week.
- **When to weed**: Best to weed after watering your containers; this makes them much easier to get out.
- **How to weed**: Gently loosen the soil around the weed with a hand fork then pull the weed out, including the root.
- **Roots**: Be careful when loosening soil around crops with shallow roots so that you don't damage them.
- **Nip them in the bud**: If you don't let the weeds develop your job will be easier and your crops will be healthier.

Temperature

Although you shouldn't plant most crops outdoors until all risks of frost have passed, the beauty of container gardening is that you have much more control over the environment. If a frost is forecast after you have planted out you can take action to prevent any damage. Remember to:

- **Insulate your pot with some Hessian or bubble wrap.**
- **Move pots to a more protected area, such as against a south-facing wall.**
- **Cover your plants with cloches to help retain heat in the soil.**
- **Move pots indoors if possible.**
- **Remember to take off any protective coverings during the day to allow your plants to get the light they need.**

Extending the Season

On a large garden plot there are plenty of ways to extend the growing season such as using greenhouses and cold frames. If you only have a small container garden it's unlikely you have space for these as well. There are, however, a few ways you can successfully sow earlier or keep your harvest going for longer.

Wrapping

Just as you'd put on a warm jacket to go out on a cold day, you can do the same with your containers to help keep the soil warmer for longer. Any material can be used to insulate the pot such as Hessian sacking, old blankets and even plastic bubble wrap. Place your chosen material around the pot tightly and secure it with string. Even though most terracotta pots are frost resistant, it's wise to treat them carefully. Ensure their bases are up off the ground during winter to prevent risks of cracking.

Sheltering

Plants left in exposed sites can suffer from cold, frost, rain and wind damage. High winds can blow pots over, resulting in plants becoming uprooted or broken. Too much rain can batter plants, rot fruit and damage leaves. Sudden cold spells and night frosts can finish the growing season for most crops. By moving containers to a south-facing wall or fence you can protect from many adverse weather conditions. You can also install windbreaks to lessen the effects of wind damage.

Cloches

Cloches are a dome or bell-shaped covering used to protect plants. They are a quick, easy way to help retain soil heat as they act like a mini greenhouse. Cloches were traditionally made from glass, which you can still buy, but most cloches are made from plastic which is cheaper. Although most are bell or semi- circular you can now buy lots of shapes and sizes including ones that look like polytunnels. You can use them in early spring to warm up the soil before planting or in late summer to protect small plants from frost damage.

Fleece

You can buy insulating fleece in a range of thicknesses. Horticultural fleece is a permeable mesh material which is soft and light. You simply drape it over your plants and pots to protect from adverse weather conditions such as frost and hail. It is easy to lay over plants and remove again. Being easy to remove is essential as you don't want to leave plants under there for too long; they need as much light as possible, plus pests like warm places too!

Fleece Jackets

Fleece plant jackets are a practical alternative to fleece. If you want to put fleece around tall plants you have to put canes in the pot then attach the fleece to them where it often comes off during the night. Fleece jackets come in a range of sizes and have zips and drawstrings which you use to completely wrap a container and its contents.

Did You Know?

The average person in the UK eats 5.9 gm (13 lbs) carrots per year.

Pot Jackets

Pot jackets are another way to insulate pots against bad weather. As their name suggests, they go around the pot and make a reusable alternative to wrapping pots in bubble wrap or sacking. They are held in place with Velcro and drawstring and can be used to protect one large pot or a group of smaller pots. Pot jackets are made from the same insulating material as people use to keep greenhouses warm during the winter.

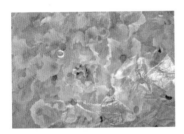

Polythene

You can buy sheets of aerated polythene to help ripen strawberries, chillies and tomatoes. This material, which you cut to size, can be left on your plants throughout the growing season and is especially useful late in the season or if you live in a colder area. It's a bit like having a portable greenhouse on your tiny plot! Due to the holes, it's OK to leave the polythene on your plants because it allows pollinating insects, air and moisture to circulate. You'll need to take it off to water your plants, but it's easy to move around.

Polytunnels

Unless you are using a raised bed, you may not have room for polytunnels, however they are now available in more sizes than ever before. It's also pretty straightforward to make your own small polytunnels by using aerated polythene sheeting. Polythene keeps plants and the soil warm, keeps off some pests such as birds but still allows light to get to your plants. By warming up soil prior to the sowing season in a raised bed, you can benefit from earlier sowing than your neighbours.

Moving Pots

The beauty of a container garden is that it's completely mobile! Although a heavy terracotta pot filled with soil will be virtually impossible to move, containers on wheels can be transported and small containers can be carried to another place. If you find yourself caught out on a frosty evening with no wrapping material or cloches to hand, then moving your pots indoors, perhaps into a shed or porch, is another way to protect from frost and ensure your plant keeps bearing food.

Did You Know?

Seed tapes are ideal for beginners – lengths of paper with seeds stuck on at regular intervals.

Protecting Crops

There are numerous ways suited to all budgets to keep your pots warm in order to extend the season. Here are some of them:

- Insulate your pots for free with old bubble wrap or blankets.
- Move containers to a south-facing wall to protect from adverse weather.
- Cloches are a good way to warm soil up at the beginning of the season.
- Fleece can be draped over pots to keep soil warm.
- Fleece jackets and pot jackets are a convenient way to keep your crops, soil and containers free from frost.
- Covering crops in aerated polythene can help ripen tender crops such as strawberries and peppers.
- If your containers are light enough or on wheels you can move them to a garage, shed or indoors.

Checklist

Here's a quick reminder of how to grow successfully:

- **Materials**: Do you have everything you need for sowing – seeds, containers and compost?

- **Location**: Have you decided to sow in situ, or in seed trays, multi-cells or individual pots?

- **Compost**: Have you prepared your compost or do you need to mix up a potting compost of your own?

- **Seedlings**: Do you have time to thin out seedlings in a seed tray or would it be best for you to sow in individual pots?

- **Windowsills**: Do you have a couple of windowsills suitable for growing seedlings?

- **Containers**: Do you have containers in a few different sizes for potting on and transplanting?

- **Hardening off**: Have you scheduled hardening off into your weekly plan so you can give your plants the best chance of survival?

- **Watering**: Are you available first thing in the morning or early evening to water your plants or would an irrigation system be useful to you?

- **Fertilizer**: Have you decided which fertilizer would be best for your needs?

- **Weeding**: When can you weed? Does 10 minutes a day or a couple of longer sessions per week suit you?

- **Longer life**: How can you extend your season? Do you have suitable wrapping materials?

Harvesting

When to Harvest

Harvesting is one of the most exciting times in the gardening year. It's great to see tiny seedlings pushing their way through the soil, but your taste of the first crop is something you cannot match! By harvesting well you can enjoy more of your hard efforts and reduce food waste.

When are Crops Ready?

If you're used to buying fresh foods from a supermarket or store you may never have seen a vegetable growing in the soil. How do you know when it's ready for picking? How can you tell

that moment of perfect ripeness? Does the plant give you any clues about harvesting? What happens if you're too early or too late?

Plant Talk

Fortunately, you'll see all sorts of signs in the food world that they are ready for picking and eating. Some plants, such as garlic and onions have foliage that wilts. With potatoes when the flowers start to die the potatoes are ready for lifting. With other plants such as tomatoes, you'll get to notice and appreciate the moment when peak ripeness has occurred due to colour and scent.

Too Early

If you pick crops before they are ripe you won't get the best result. Some foods such as tomatoes will ripen off the vine, but they don't taste as good as they do when picked fresh. Some crops don't ripen well at all once they are picked, so it's best to leave them on the plant to reach maturity. With potatoes, for example, you'll get smaller potatoes and less of them, which is a shame after you've taken the time to grow them.

Too Late

Picking crops too late is in many ways worse than picking too early. If you leave them too late you might miss out altogether because there will be pests such as wasps or slugs

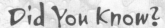

Did You Know?

Pears should be harvested when they are mature, but still hard, and ripened off the tree for best eating qualities.

that will happily munch your harvest. With some crops such as courgettes, leaving them on the plant means they soon turn to marrows. If you miss a runner bean on the plant and leave it, it can 'switch off' the growing energy and stop the plant producing new beans. Leaving beetroot and radishes in the ground can turn them woody, while leaving lettuces and spinach can lead to 'bolting' which means your crop becomes unusable.

Harvesting Reminders

Once you've spent the season tending to your crops, there is nothing like harvest time! Coming in from the garden with home-grown produce is such a wonderful feeling, but how do you know when your food is ready? Here are some hints:

- Some plants have foliage which turns yellow and wilts when it's ready such as garlic.
- Some foods need to be picked before they are ripe e.g. pears.
- Other foods are best picked at the peak of ripeness, such as tomatoes.
- Timing is everything; too soon and foods won't taste their best, too late and the food can rot.
- The prime goal of a plant is to reproduce; if you allow bean pods to mature on the bush or basil to set seed it will prevent new growth, so harvest regularly.

Fresh is Best

As well as observing when crops are ready to be picked, well-timed harvesting involves bearing in mind when you will be eating them. For the best taste you want to eat your food as soon after picking it as possible. You could even enjoy an outdoor buffet in summer; take a plate and walk around your plants taking a few salad leaves, uprooting some radishes, picking fresh tomatoes off the vine and adding a few herbs. You'll never have tasted a better meal! Once you pick foods, the natural sugars rapidly start to turn to starch which alters the texture and taste of your food.

Advantages of Fresh Food

There are many advantages to eating food, picked ripe, straight from the plant:

- **Taste**: Nothing can beat freshly picked, ripe produce for taste.
- **Nutrition**: Nutritional content starts to deteriorate as soon as you pick food; eating it fresh means you get the biggest benefit to your health.
- **Yield**: Regular picking means the plant keeps producing new food.

Disadvantages of Fresh Food

There aren't many disadvantages to eating fresh food straight from the plant, but here are some:

- **Inconvenience**: Not always practical to pick and eat there and then, especially if you are busy.
- **Difficult timing**: If you can only tend to your garden a couple of times a week, you might miss the peak of ripeness.
- **Surplus**: You can't eat a glut of produce in one go.

Top Tip

Pull up carrots before winter otherwise they can get frost damaged. Alternatively, many root crops can be over-wintered in the garden as long as you protect the soil from freezing.

Storing Food

It's not always practical to eat food straight away; perhaps you need to keep it for two or three days before using. In this case knowing how to store foods for freshness will save you wasting your precious produce. Some foods need to be stored at room temperature, whereas others will benefit from being kept in the refrigerator. Some foods need no preparation to store them, whereas others need a little preparation beforehand.

Different Storage for Different Crops

Not all foods like to be stored in the fridge. For example bananas go black and potatoes rapidly increase the amount of sugar they contain when refrigerated which can result in a sickly sweet meal.

Tomatoes shouldn't be refrigerated until they are fully ripe and should be brought back to room temperature before eating. Other foods store well in the refrigerator and benefit from cooler temperatures to prevent spoilage.

Lettuce and Salad Leaves

Lettuce is best eaten fresh but you can store it for around five days in the refrigerator. When you've picked or cut your leaves, wash them in cold water to dislodge any soil. Drain well and when most of the water has drained off wrap the leaves in paper towels and place in a paper bag. Store in a salad crisper or keep them in a container of cold water. Put the container in the refrigerator where they will stay fresh.

Leafy Greens

Spinach, kale and chard can get gritty, so they need washing well. Separate the leaves and wash in a bowl of water. Dry well and put in a plastic bag. Kale will keep for up to a week, whereas spinach and chard will keep for about four days.

Tomatoes

Tomatoes need to be kept at room temperature otherwise you lose the flavour. If they are not quite ripe, they will ripen in the warmth of your house. They don't need to be kept in direct sunlight; a shelf in a warm room or kitchen work surface is perfect. Store them in a bowl and use ripe tomatoes within a couple of days.

Onions and Garlic

Onions and garlic store really well in a dark, cool place with plenty of air circulation. Hang them up in a net; an old fruit net is ideal and suspend from the ceiling in a cool room such as a garage. Stored like this, without any damp getting to them, they will keep for over a month.

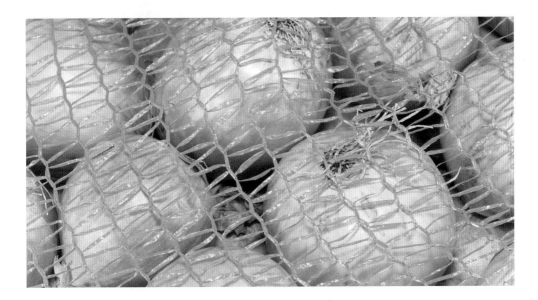

Potatoes

It's unlikely you'll be growing maincrop potatoes in containers, but new potatoes need to be eaten quickly after harvest. The best place for storage is in the soil, so leave them until you are ready to eat them. If you bring in too many, put the excess ones in a paper bag and keep in a cool, dark place. Once light gets to them, they can turn green and then they shouldn't be eaten.

Root Crops

Carrots and beetroot store well in a cool, dark place. Some people keep them in the refrigerator but they can rot quite quickly once they get damp. On the other hand, if they get too dry they can go soft! Traditionally carrots are stored in trays of sand, so it might be best to leave them in the soil until you want to eat them or store in the refrigerator and use within a week. Both beetroot and carrots store better with the tops removed. Don't forget you can eat beetroot tops; use them as an alternative to spinach. Avoid washing root crops until you want to eat them since the moisture can encourage rotting.

Did You Know?

Carrot tops are rich in chlorophyll and vitamin K – chop them into salads or add to soups.

Herbs

Treat herbs like cut flowers. Cut a length of stem and put them in a small jar of water. They will store like this on your kitchen work surface for three or four days. Take the herbs you want and snip them fresh into your meals. If you have a tiny kitchen and work surface space is limited, you can treat herbs like lettuce – wash and dry them, then store in plastic bags in the refrigerator.

Short-term Freshness

If you're not ready to eat your food straight away, you can store it for a few days in your home. Whether you store in the refrigerator or counter top depends on the food:

- Bananas, potatoes and tomatoes should not be stored in the refrigerator.
- Some crops such as herbs can be stored like cut flowers in a jar of cold water.
- Wash salad leaves before storing in plastic bags and allow a few drops of water to cling onto the leaves to keep them crisp.
- Store root crops in a cool, dark place for a few days before eating.
- Remove the tops from beetroot and carrots before storing for best results.
- Store potatoes in the dark otherwise they can turn green and then you can't eat them.

Top Tip

If you have a glut of something that you want to freeze, a vacuum sealer is a worthwhile investment.

Advantages of Short-term Storage

Good short-term storage is a way to prolong the life of harvested foods. There are many advantages including:

- Food stored carelessly can go off within a few hours, but when stored well can be good for longer.
- Picking and storing food for a few days saves time when preparing meals.
- Having food stored for a few days encourages you to eat a wider range of foods.
- Reduces overall food waste.

Disadvantages of Short-term Storage

Storing food for a few days is a great way to reduce food waste but it's not without its disadvantages:

- It can take time to wash and sort crops such as salad leaves for storing; it might be quicker to pick and eat as required.
- Taste and texture start to deteriorate once food is picked off the plant.
- If you store too much food it can go off before you use it all.

Top Tip

To keep fruit at its freshest, do not store next to bananas. Bananas give off ethylene which causes other fruits to ripen and rot more quickly.

Drying Food

Drying is one of the oldest forms of food preservation and has been around for thousands of years. Bacteria live and breed in wet conditions, so removing the water content of food means the food can be preserved for a long time. You've probably come across dried fruit or herbs in the supermarket and there is no reason why you can't do the same yourself at home.

Why Dry Food?

Although traditionally dried in the sun, you can dry food inside your home; either by air, oven or by using an electric dehydrator. Drying food alters the texture but can enhance the flavour. Dried vegetables make useful additions to winter soups and stews.

Advantages of Drying

There are several reasons why drying food has been popular for so long:

- Dried foods can last for a few months when stored properly.
- Flavour can be enhanced as dried food becomes more concentrated.
- Dried foods take up little storage room.
- Dried vegetables make a useful addition to winter soups and stews.

Disadvantages of Drying

Although it's one of the oldest forms of food storage, there are some disadvantages to drying food:

- If you're using an electric dehydrator or oven, it can take a long time to prepare the foods.
- Using electricity for drying costs more than air drying.
- Apart from air drying which is left to take care of itself, once you start the drying process you can't leave it; so you need to be in all day.
- Unless you get all foods cut in uniform sizes they don't all dry at the same rate; you need to be watching throughout the drying process.

What to Dehydrate

Almost all herbs dry successfully as rows of supermarket shelves will show! Most fruits dry well, especially apples and pears and the following vegetables also dry successfully:

- Beetroot
- Carrots
- Peppers and chillies
- Onions
- Courgettes
- Mushrooms

Step-by-step Drying

It is crucial to only use food in perfect condition. If something is starting to decompose it needs using straight away, not preserving. Drying is a straightforward process; just follow these steps for an electric dehydrator or oven. The method is slightly different if air drying:

- After selecting good quality food, wash and deseed it.
- Some foods such as apples and pears will need to be peeled. Other foods such as courgettes can be dried in slices with skins on.
- Cut foods into small, thin slices; the thinner the better. Smaller pieces contain less moisture and will dry quicker.
- If you want to preserve the colour of apples and pears, dunk them in a bowl of water and lemon juice while you chop the rest of the fruits.
- Place your prepared fruits and vegetables onto drying racks and start the drying process either in an oven or electric dehydrator.

Oven Drying

To dry food in an oven, follow these steps:

- Set your oven to the lowest temperature, preferably around 60°C (140°F).
- Leave the oven door open by about 4 in to ensure air can circulate.
- Set the oven trays about 2–3 in apart.
- Place the vegetables and fruit without them touching onto food trays.
- Racks are ideal, but you can use solid–based biscuit trays (cookie sheets).
- Place the food trays on the oven shelves and let them slowly dry out.
- Depending on the water content of the food this can take anything from two to 10 hours.

- Keep checking the food and turning it if necessary; you want it to dry out, not cook.
- Cool the food thoroughly before storing in labelled, dated containers.

Electric Dehydrators

A dehydrator is an electrical appliance designed to make food drying simple. It produces heat at around 60°C (140°F), has built in ventilation and contains a fan to keep air circulating around the food. Each product will come with manufacturers' guidelines about the length of time needed for certain foods and how to use it, but the basic guidelines are:

- Prepare food and cut into thin slices as outlined previously.
- Blanch vegetables by placing in boiling water for a couple of minutes then plunging into ice cold water to stop the cooking process. Cool and dry.
- Place food, spaced out, on the dehydrator trays.
- Stack trays into the dehydrator and switch on.
- Dehydrate fruits until they are still moist and chewy and dehydrate vegetables until they are really dry and almost brittle.

Air drying

Air drying works really well for herbs and chillies. It costs nothing to do and requires little attention. The most important thing is to make sure the humidity is low in the room you are using and the room is well ventilated. Here is how to dry herbs:

Top Tip

Harvest beans when they are young and tender to keep them producing new pods.

- Cut long stems of herbs when they are dry – around midday is a good time to harvest them.
- Tie them in bundles with string; around six stems per bundle.
- Cover the heads of the herbs with a paper bag – this prevents them getting covered in dust or shedding bits on your floor.
- Suspend the herb stems from the ceiling, away from direct sunlight.
- Check the herbs after about four to six weeks to see if they are dry and crumbly.
- Crumble the leaves into small containers – label, date and store in a cool, dry place.

Did you know?

Tomatoes lose colour, firmness and flavour if stored in the refrigerator.

Using Dehydrated Foods

Dried apple rings and pear slices are a delicious and healthy snack while berries are a useful addition for baking or smoothies. Dried vegetables need to be rehydrated in water for a couple of hours before cooking. They will swell up to their original size and are best used in recipes with a lot of liquid such as a casserole or stew. Dried herbs can be added to dishes for the last few minutes of cooking time to release their essential oils.

Freezing and Preserving Food

Most vegetables and fruits can be frozen very successfully to preserve your harvest; in fact, it is one of the most common ways to preserve crops. A quick and simple process, you don't need any special equipment apart from a few things you may already have at home, such as freezer bags and plastic containers with lids. You can store vegetables and fruits for up to a year this way. The beauty of freezing is that you can retain a high nutritional content.

Why Freeze?

There are many advantages to freezing, making it an ideal way to preserve your harvest:

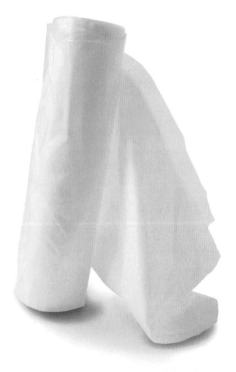

- ✔ **A wide range of foods can be frozen.**
- ✔ **Freezing retains nutrients.**
- ✔ **Does not require any special equipment.**
- ✔ **Quick and simple process.**
- ✔ **Freezing retains the structure, flavour and texture of fresh foods unlike pickling.**

Disadvantages of Freezing

There are a few disadvantages to freezing, outlined below:

- **Not everyone has a large freezer.**
- **Ongoing cost of keeping a freezer running compared to canning which requires only a shelf to keep things fresh.**
- **Risk of freezer burn if you do not wrap and store correctly.**
- **If your freezer goes wrong and it's full of your harvest, you'll lose it all; there is no risk of this with canning or drying.**

Not for Freezers

Some foods are not really suitable for freezing because they collapse and become mushy. Strawberries, courgettes and tomatoes all lose their structure and when they defrost they turn to mush. However, you can freeze them in meals or use bananas and strawberries in smoothies. Courgettes can be made into ratatouille and then frozen. Tomatoes can be made into soup and frozen into portions.

Before You Start

A few hours before you start preparing vegetables and fruits for freezing you need to set the temperature of your freezer as low as possible. This is because successful freezing depends on how quickly you can reduce the temperature of the food. The slower the food freezes, the more the flavour and nutritional content will be affected. The faster you freeze it the least bacteria is able to survive, meaning your frozen produce is healthy and safe.

Freezer Containers

It's vital that the container you choose to freeze food is moisture proof. The idea is to keep moisture in the product and keep air out. The two types of materials most commonly used for home freezing are plastic bags or rigid plastic containers. Flexible freezer bags are suitable for products with little or no liquid and should have as much air as possible squeezed out before freezing the product. Rigid containers are especially good for 'wetter' produce such as fruits packed in syrup and should have a tight-fitting lid.

Blanching

Although some people try to skimp on this step, it makes a lot of difference to your enjoyment of the frozen crop. Blanching not only retains colour but it preserves the texture and flavour of the food while keeping vitamin C levels high. Successful blanching is all in the timing. The idea is to get vegetables as hot as possible as quickly as you can before cooling them quickly in water. Once they are cool, you can pack and freeze them.

Did You Know?

Parsnips need a frost in order to develop their best taste.

How to Blanch

Using the largest container you have – a preserving pan, stock pot or your biggest saucepan – bring water to the boil. You'll need about six pints of water to 0.45 kg (1lb) of vegetables. Plunge your prepared vegetables into the water and bring it back to a rolling boil as quickly as you can; then maintain that temperature for around two to three minutes.

Draining and Cooling

Drain the vegetables and cool them quickly to stop the cooking process. The easiest way to do this is to hold them in a sieve or colander and plunge this into a bowl of iced water. Once the food has cooled down, remove it from the water, drain and dry the food before packing into freezer bags or containers. Label the container and place in your freezer.

Blanching Times

Here are some blanching times to give you an idea of the work involved with freezing foods:

- **Topped, tailed and sliced beans**: 2–3 minutes.
- **Small whole beetroot**: 5–10 minutes.
- **Sliced carrots**: 3–5 minutes.
- **Sliced onions**: 2 minutes.
- **Parsnip strips**: 2 minutes.
- **Pepper slices**: 3 minutes.
- **Spinach**: 2 minutes.

Quick Freezing

If you only have a few vegetables for freezing and you will use them within two or three months you can miss out the blanching step. To do this you'll need to freeze the produce on trays. Chop the vegetables into dice or slices, put a thin layer onto a tray and freeze. Once the fruit or vegetables are frozen, pour into portion-sized freezer bags.

Good Labelling

There is nothing worse than going to your freezer and pulling out packs of UFOs (unidentified frozen objects). We all think we will remember what we have put into each bag or container as we prepare it, but once we've done it a few times and a few ice crystals have formed on the outside of things, it's easy to forget what's in each pack or container! Putting food without dates into the freezer can result in spoilage and waste. You might find things in the back of the freezer and not know if it is still good to eat so end up throwing it away unnecessarily.

How Long to Freeze?

Most fruits and vegetables, if prepared well, will look and taste good for up to a year once frozen. You should think about preserving enough produce to last you until that food is available fresh from your garden again otherwise you will end up with a build-up of frozen foods; a bit like a glut in your freezer! Make sure you rotate foods well, bringing older stuff to the front and putting newer foods at the back. Longer storage of fruits and vegetables will not make the food unfit for use, but will decrease its quality.

Preserving and Bottling

Preserving and bottling (also known as 'canning') are other effective methods of storing food. However, unless you have a large glut of something it's probably not worth making pickles and chutneys or going to the trouble of heating and sterilizing just a few jars for bottling.

Chutney

Making chutney is one of the most straightforward ways to use up a glut of onions, apples and marrows and most people have a favourite chutney recipe. Chutney is a spicy condiment made of chopped fruits or vegetables cooked in vinegar, sugar, ginger and spices which have an Indian origin. In the UK, chutney is used as an accompaniment to salads, added to cheese sandwiches and stirred through stews to enrich the taste. You're limited only by your imagination when making chutney, but one of the most popular recipes amongst gardeners is green tomato chutney.

Riverford's Green Tomato Chutney Recipe

Making green tomato chutney is easy enough but it does take some time to prepare the ingredients. You need a large pan and should allow a few hours for it to be ready. Save up old jam jars throughout the year to reduce your costs. Sterilize jars and lids by first washing them, then boiling them in water for 10 minutes (use metal lids only if they have a plastic lining to stop the vinegar reacting with the metal). You will need the following ingredients to make this recipe, which is from Riverford, an organic produce delivery service:

 750 g (1 lb 10 oz) green tomatoes, washed and chopped
 350 g (12 oz) shallots or onions, peeled and chopped
 200 g (7 oz) cooking apples, peeled, cored and chopped
 300 ml (½ pint) malt vinegar

small piece root ginger, peeled

  a few yellow mustard seeds (optional)

2 red chillies

 100 g (3½) oz raisins

1 tsp salt

200 g (7 oz) brown sugar

Put the tomatoes, shallots or onions and the apples in a large, heavy-based pan with half the vinegar. Bring to the boil, then gently cook for about 30 minutes, until tender. Tie the chillies, root ginger and mustard seeds (if using) in a muslin bag, bruise with a heavy rolling pin or hammer and add to the pan with the raisins. Cook on a low heat, stirring from time to time until the mixture thickens (about 1 hour). Add the salt, sugar and the rest of the vinegar, stirring well until the sugar dissolves. Continue cooking until the mixture has thickened. Remove the muslin spice bag. Pot into sterilized jars while the chutney is still warm. Seal. Leave for 6 weeks to mature.

Tomato Ketchup Recipe

Tomato ketchup is a popular condiment and is simple to make. Once you've made your own, you'll never go back to buying shop bought again! Here's a recipe for one small bottle of tomato ketchup:

 1 kg (2¼) lb tomatoes

 1 small onion, finely chopped

 ½ small red pepper, finely chopped

 2 tbsp brown sugar

1 tbsp cider vinegar

 ¼ tsp dried garlic

 ⅛ tsp dried cinnamon

 ⅛ tsp allspice

 ¼ tsp ground mustard

 1 tsp paprika

Place the tomatoes onion and pepper into a pan with a well-fitting lid and cook over a gentle heat until soft. Sieve into a clean saucepan and add the remaining ingredients. Cook over a gentle heat without a lid until the sauce has thickened to the desired consistency. Pour into an old glass ketchup bottle that you have sterilized. Label and date your sauce.

Checklist

Some things to consider before storing the fruit of your crops:

- **Storage**: Which methods of food storage appeal most to you?

- **Stay fresh**: Picking food fresh from the plant and eating it straight away is healthier and tastes better. The more moisture a food contains, the quicker it decomposes or wilts, so try and pick salad leaves just before you want to eat them.

- **Ripeness**: Check signs of perfect ripeness daily – on hot days food can ripen quickly.

- **Quick storing**: Short-term storage is ideal if you've picked too much food; check whether you need refrigerator space or if foods should be kept at room temperature.

- **Drying**: This is one of the oldest methods of food preservation; can you air or oven dry or would you prefer to buy a dehydrator?

- **Freezing**: When freezing foods, set the temperature to its lowest setting a few hours before you start preparing your foods.

- **Blanching**: Remember to blanch vegetables before freezing or dehydrating.

- **Gluts**: If you keep getting a glut of something, consider successive sowing throughout the year and find some nice chutney or pickle recipes to make the most of your excess food.

Pests & Problems

Pests Large and Small

You are unlikely to be bothered by large pests such as pigeons, rabbits and cats in a container garden although the odd tenacious squirrel might find his way into your planters and have a dig around in the soil for something to eat. Squirrels are attracted to bird feeders so try and keep these away from your containers. Cats may get into larger planters, especially raised beds full of soft compost as this makes the perfect toilet. You can deter them with citrus sprays or sprinkle cinnamon or cloves around the area.

Aphids

The aphid family includes greenfly and blackfly. They insert their sharp, syringe-like mouths into plants and suck out the sap which can weaken the plant and spread disease. After they have fed, aphids leave a sticky residue on the plant called honeydew which can in turn attract ants. Marching ants on your plants may alert you to an aphid infestation. There are several effective ways of dealing with aphids. As they are easy to spot prevention of an infestation is definitely better than cure. Try some of the following:

Remove the Growing Tips

Blackfly are particularly fond of the tips of broad beans. If you are growing broad beans you can physically remove the blackfly by taking off the mature growing tip when the beans start to pod. Destroy the blackfly covered tip otherwise they will move on to something else they like such as lettuce.

> ### Top Tip
> **A few aphids can be rubbed off the plant with your thumb and forefinger.**

Spraying

You can control a small population of aphids by hosing or spraying them off with water every few days. If you add a drop of regular dishwashing liquid it will be even more effective or you can buy insecticidal soft soap for this purpose. Spray in the morning so the leaves have chance to dry before night fall.

Predators

There is nothing a ladybird loves more to eat than aphids, so try and attract them to your garden. Ladybirds lay their eggs in nettles, so leave a patch in the corner of your plot. If you're growing food without a garden such as on a balcony or in window boxes you can buy ladybirds online to introduce into your space! Parasitic wasps and lacewings also feed off aphids so introduce them into your garden.

Sacrificial Plants

In companion gardening, one of the methods used for natural pest control is sacrificial planting. Nasturtiums are commonly used as a sacrificial plant for aphids because they love them. Try planting them next to the plants that are troubled by aphids and see if they go to the nasturtiums instead.

Cabbage Whites

Although you may not be growing full-sized cabbages in your small container garden, the cabbage white butterfly loves nothing more than some kale leaves and can become a real pest, even in the smallest of gardens. The adult butterflies lay eggs on the underside of leaves and the ensuing caterpillars bore holes in the leaves and can leave nothing for you to eat.

Top Tip

Plants like spearmint and fennel attract insects that feed on aphids, so grow them in a small container.

Daily Checks and Prevention

If you see cabbage white butterflies around your plants, check daily underneath leaves for the eggs and caterpillars. Be sure to pick them off before any damage occurs. Covering plants with horticultural fleece will prevent the eggs being laid in the first place and this is ideal for plants such as kale or cabbages.

Did You Know?

The cabbage white butterfly can fly over 100 miles in its lifetime!

Dealing with Cabbage Whites

These yellow and black caterpillars can eat holes in leaves and reduce your plant to nothing in a very short time. If you see the cabbage white butterfly around your plants it's time for you to go out and inspect what's going on – prevention is better than cure. Get into the habit of checking your plants daily; look at the underside of leaves and take off any eggs or caterpillars. If you cannot check daily, then use horticultural fleece to prevent eggs being laid.

Carrot Fly

The carrot fly can smell carrots from half a mile away! It lays its eggs and the larva bore holes into the roots which can make the carrots almost inedible. However, there are several ways to stop carrot fly destroying your crop.

Masking

You can put the fly off by masking the scent of the crops it loves with members of the allium family. Chives are ideal in a small container garden but you do need roughly as many chive plants as carrot plants, so this might not be practical except in large containers. Garlic is another member of the allium family that can be planted alongside carrots.

Garlic plants alongside carrot plants may help deter carrot fly.

Fleece

By rolling horticultural fleece over the top of the soil once you have sown your carrot seed you will form a barrier against the carrot fly. You'll need to peg the fleece down and leave it in place. You only need to remove the fleece when harvesting the carrots as it allows light and water to get through.

Barriers

The carrot fly cannot fly very high so a physical barrier will stop it getting to your crop. One of the easiest ways with a container garden is to sow carrots in a container that is high off the ground, such as a large pot or one that is on a frame. Alternatively a window box with short-rooted carrots is ideal. If your containers are on the ground then a net windbreaker fixed around the container should work.

The carrots in the large pot here will be better protected from carrot fly than their lower companions, but all would benefit from being raised further off the ground.

Sowing Times

The carrot fly is around in the middle of the spring when most people do the majority of their sowing. If you can postpone your sowing time until later in the year such as late spring or early summer, you'll be sowing out of sync with the carrot fly's breeding cycle and so should avoid problems.

Careful Sowing

The carrot fly is attracted to the scent released by the feathery carrot leaves; one of the best ways to prevent carrot fly is to handle the seedlings very carefully. If at all possible, sow so thinly that you never need to thin your seedlings as when you do you can bruise the delicate leaves and release the scent. When you water your carrots, try not to disturb the leaves or batter them with the force of the water. Some varieties of carrot are more resistant to carrot fly than others. Try planting 'Resistafly', 'Sytan' or 'Fly Away'.

Did You Know?

The carrot fly can attack carrot, parsnip and parsley.

Red Spider Mite

Red spider mites enjoy hot, dry summers and will thrive indoors, so look out for these if you are growing your garden inside your home. Prevention is definitely better than cure with this pest because they are very resistant to control and can do a lot of damage, including weakening plants so much they die. You often see signs of damage before you see the mites; they make 'webbing' on the underside of old leaves and you might see mottling on lower leaves. Mite damage occurs on old, lower leaves before new, succulent growth.

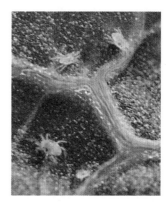

Humidity

Your best defence against the red spider mite is climate control. They thrive in hot, dry climates, so alter your climate by keeping plants humid. Indoors you can spray with a plant mister and outdoors make sure you regularly water your plants. Red spider mites are not such a big problem outdoors, but they are worth looking out for if your climate supports them.

Removing Spider Mites

Be aware that red spider mites are pretty resistant to control. If you spot them in time, they can be removed from the leaf surface before they build webbing and start damaging your plants. Give the underside of your plant's lower leaves a weekly blast of water. You can add insecticide soap or regular dishwashing soap if you have an infestation already.

Slugs

Slugs are one of the most common and most hated garden pests. They munch through the leaves of your plants at night-time and can reduce seedlings and young plants to nothing. It's not unusual to get up in the morning and find an entire row of small plants eaten.

Mature Plants

Slugs are pretty lazy and favour soft, tender young plants and seedlings. One way to prevent slug damage is to sow seeds and transplant them indoors, then move mature, larger plants to their final container.

Did You Know?
Slugs have four noses!

Barriers

The use of cloches over young plants is one way to keep slugs away. Alternatively, people have had mixed results by putting sharp items around their plants such as gravel, crushed eggshells or bark. Other solutions are to place copper tape around plants as slugs don't like going over it.

Traps

Slugs are fond of beer and one popular method of keeping your crops free of slugs is to lay beer traps. These are shallow containers half filled with beer, sunk into the soil near your plants. The slugs will be attracted to the beer and fall in. Once they fall in they will drown and you can dispose of them in the morning.

Keeping it tidy

Slugs like untidy gardens where they can hide! You should never be meticulous with your gardening; it's all about balance, but clearing away old plant growth and weeds give slugs fewer places to hide.

Predators

Slugs have plenty of natural predators including frogs, hedgehogs and ducks. While it might not be practical to entice ducks in your garden, frogs and hedgehogs can be encouraged to have a good meal.

Slug Pellets

You can buy numerous types of slug pellets from garden centres and online. Sprinkle them around plants that are particularly vulnerable to slugs such as young, tender shoots. It's best to use these as a last resort because they can be toxic to other animals (including their natural predators), pets and young children.

Diseases

Diseases in plants can wipe out your entire crop, so you need to be vigilant and act quickly if you see any signs of damage. Swift action can often stop a disease in its tracks and prevent untold damage.

Blight

Blight was one of the contributors to the Irish famine back in 1845. Blight affects potatoes and tomatoes and will rapidly destroy the entire crop. On potatoes, the leaves and stems turn brown and rot and the tubers go soggy and smell bad. Tomatoes have similar markings on the leaves while the fruit may show brown patches before decaying. Blight is caused by a fungus-like organism.

Potato Blight

Blight is most common in wet weather so a warm, wet summer can be disastrous for the spreading of this disease. Once you have it, you need to act quickly to stop it spreading. Any

infected plants should be removed and burned straight away. If the disease has not reached the tubers, you may be able to dig them up and use them. Maincrop potatoes are more susceptible to blight than early varieties, and it's unlikely you would be growing maincrop varieties in a small container garden, so the risk is small.

Tomato Blight

Tomatoes tend to suffer from blight more than potatoes. If you see signs of it, remove and burn any diseased plants. If the tomatoes are OK, you can harvest them and ripen them off indoors. You can apply fungicides following manufacturers' guidelines. Tomatoes grown indoors are at much less risk from developing blight than those grown outdoors.

Blossom End Rot

Although it can look unsightly, and while there is nothing you can do to save damaged crops, you still have time to save the rest of the crop from becoming affected. Blossom end rot occurs in crops such as aubergines, tomatoes and peppers and can be seen as a black sunken patch on the end of the fruit.

Careful Watering

Blossom end rot is not a disease per se; it's a symptom of irregular watering which leads to a calcium deficiency. Unfortunately for container gardeners, plants grown in growbags or containers are more likely to suffer from blossom end rot than those grown in an open plot of soil. You can prevent blossom end rot with regular and consistent watering and never allowing the pot to dry out.

Botrytis

Botrytis is a fungal infection that causes grey mould and brown spots. It can affect any plant but strawberries and tomatoes are often affected because they are soft. Botrytis can affect all parts of the plant above the ground and you'll often see dead brown patches on leaves or stems before the mould appears.

Mechanical Control

The quickest way to prevent botrytis spreading is to pick off the infected parts of the plant and destroy them. Make sure you do this on a dry day to prevent spreading the disease. Prevent the botrytis spores surviving throughout the autumn by clearing away plant debris and keeping all containers and tools clean.

Did You Know?

Approximately one million people died and a million more emigrated from Ireland during the great famine.

Keeping Things Dry

Fungal spores spread most rapidly during times of high humidity and cool temperatures. If you get a few days of spring rain you should look out for signs of botrytis on your plants. One way to prevent strawberries getting botrytis is to keep the fruits up off the soil; you could use straw for this.

Fungicides

Fungicides for dealing with botrytis are available online and in garden centres. Follow the manufacturers' recommendations. If you are gardening organically you can make your own anti-fungal sprays using the plant horsetail or neem oil.

Healthy Plants

Botrytis tends to favour weakened or unhealthy plants, so by keeping your crop in good condition you should lessen the risk of this fungal infection taking hold. Make sure you don't plant crops too closely together to help reduce the humidity and prevent infections spreading quickly.

Dealing with Botrytis

Once botrytis becomes established it can wipe out entire plants or even the whole crop, so prevention is the key. Here are some practical tips:

- **In periods of cool, wet weather, inspect plants regularly for signs of infestation.**
- **During autumn keep your containers clean and get rid of decaying plants.**
- **If you spot botrytis on a plant, remove the affected part straight away and destroy it.**
- **Keep susceptible foods such as strawberries off the surface of the soil by using straw.**
- **Keep plants happy and healthy and give them adequate space.**
- **Use synthetic or natural fungicides to help deal with an outbreak of botrytis.**

Damping Off

Damping off is a fungal disease that affects seedlings; instead of lovely rows of healthy, green seedlings you get a mass of collapsed plants covered in white fungus or you end up with nothing at all! Damping off is more prevalent when sowing seeds indoors.

Good Spacing

To reduce the risk of damping off, ensure you sow thinly. When seedlings emerge too close to one another humidity levels can rise, which increases the risk of fungal infections such as damping off. When sown indoors, keep humidity low by increasing ventilation if necessary.

Quality Compost and Water

The spores which cause damping off can live in soil, so never use garden soil for sowing seeds and always use a quality, commercial product from a reputable source. Another way damping off can be a problem is that the spores can live in water. Although it is fine to water established plants with rain water gathered in a rain barrel, seedlings should always be watered with tap water.

Hygiene

Good hygiene is the key to avoiding fungal infections such as damping off. Keep seed trays and tools scrupulously clean. Although it is recommended that you buy new seed trays every year you can get away with thorough cleaning and sterilization which is the more environmentally friendly choice. However, if you've experienced damping off, it is better to destroy those particular trays and replace them with new ones.

Top Tip

Sowing seeds too deeply can lead to damping off. The general rule is to cover the seeds with their own depth of compost.

Keep all pots and tools clean to reduce the risk of damping off.

Mildew

Powdery mildew, as the name might suggest, causes a white, powdery coating on leaves, stems and flowers. It is a fungal disease which can attack any plant and is commonly found on courgettes and cucumbers. Downy mildew can be spotted by white patches on the underside of leaves with yellow patches above and can affect both seedlings and mature plants of the brassicas family.

Fungicides

Using fungicides is a popular way to get rid of powdery mildew and it can be directed exactly where the disease has affected plants to prevent it spreading further. Specific fungicides can be bought online or from garden centres and you should follow manufacturers' recommendations for application. Organic fungicides include horsetail and neem oil (a natural pesticide). Unfortunately it is difficult to treat downy mildew at home.

Leave plenty of space between plants to encourage air flow.

Clearing Up

Sweeping up decayed plants and fallen leaves during autumn is an important method of prevention as the spores of powdery mildew can live on these and proliferate the following spring. To decrease the risk of downy mildew, leave plenty of space between plants to encourage air flow and remove diseased plants immediately then destroy them. Regular weeding can also help.

Careful Watering

To help prevent powdery mildew, soil should not become too dry and plants in containers should get adequate water. It's important to keep roots moist; you can do this by using ground cover plants or using mulches. Downy mildew, on the other hand often occurs from over watering, where the air becomes too humid, so careful watering is essential.

Top Tip
Clearing away old plant growth and weeds at the end of the season means a healthier garden.

Top Tip
Cleaning and sterilizing of pots and tools can help prevent mildew spores multiplying.

Weeds

Weeding a traditional plot can be a long and arduous chore. No sooner have you weeded one patch when another area seems rife with tiny weeds. Fortunately weeding in containers is a much quicker and easier job which will take just a few minutes a day.

Preventing Weeds

If you can prevent weeds from taking hold in the first place, your job will be easier. Choosing the right soil is crucial. Garden soil is no good for containers; it can be contaminated with weed seeds, pests and diseases and doesn't stay nutritious for long. You need commercially prepared, sterile compost for your containers.

Little and Often

Weeding little and often is the key to success. As soon as you see a tiny weed seedling, pull it out with your hands and dispose of it; no special tools required! It is essential to get weeds out before they flower otherwise they can go to seed and multiply around your garden.

Limited Supply

Remember, a container only holds a limited supply of water and nutrients so you'll need to pull weeds out as soon as you see them to prevent them competing with your plants. Left unchecked, weeds will not only take valuable water, but they will compete for light and smother or strangle your crops. Weeds can also carry harmful diseases and pests.

Don't be too hasty to get rid off all your nettles – they make great soup!

Eliminate Space

Weeds like space, so you can eliminate available space by careful planting. Large areas of exposed soil are inviting for weed seeds which get dropped by birds or carried by the wind. Although you won't have much bare soil in containers, except perhaps in raised beds, you might find the square foot gardening method works well and gives you a virtually weed-free garden.

Dealing with Weeds

Preventing weeds taking over is pretty straightforward with container gardening. Unlike traditional plots that have lots of soil for weeds to take hold, the scale of container gardening means they are much easier to deal with. Here are some suggestions:

- Never use garden soil for containers; always choose fresh, good quality compost from a reputable supplier.
- Add weeding to your weekly schedule. Do either a few minutes every day or a couple of longer stints twice a week.
- Pull out weeds when they are small to prevent them competing with plants.
- Make sure you get weeds out before they flower and set seed otherwise the problem will spread!
- By covering as much of the soil as possible with plants, you'll eliminate space for weeds to grow.

Organic Growing

Organic gardening methods minimize the use of manufactured and synthetic chemicals and favour more natural methods of pest, disease and weed control such as companion planting, paying attention to sowing times, physical barriers, biological control and regular weeding. In essence it favours a 'prevention is better than cure' approach in which the growing area is treated and respected as a full ecosystem.

Pesticides

A diet high in fresh fruit and vegetables is a healthy diet, but when sprayed with lots of pesticides, the negative effects on health and the environment can be considerable. Not so long ago ALL gardening and farming was organic. It's only during the twentieth century that a large supply of new synthetic chemicals was introduced to the food supply.

Effects on Air

Pesticides can contribute to air pollution by drifting. If you choose to spray pesticides, pick a calm day with low wind to prevent drift. Drift occurs by wind picking up pesticide particles and depositing them elsewhere. Other pesticides give off volatile organic compounds, which can react with other chemicals to form ozone. This accounts for six per cent loss of ozone layer.

Effects on Water

Pesticides pollute many streams and rivers across the world and can contaminate rain and groundwater. Pesticides end up in water by drifting when sprayed, leaching through the soil or in run-off. Once in the water, pesticides can cause devastation to aquatic life and upset the delicate eco balance. In severe cases, all the fish in a particular stream can die.

Top Tip

If you decide to use pesticides or insecticides, make sure you wear gloves, long-sleeved tops and eye protection.

Aquatic Life

Another way in which pesticides and other chemicals impact aquatic life is by killing off sources of fish food. This means that the fish move to different waters where they may be exposed to the risk of predators. Alternatively, certain chemicals kill plants in the water that then rot and use up all the oxygen in the water, causing the fish to suffocate.

Pesticides that get into watercourses can lead to the death of aquatic life.

Effects on soil

Many of the chemicals used in pesticides are persistent and remain in the soil. A persistent chemical may last for decades and adversely affect soil by decreasing the general biodiversity. This in turn means that micro-organisms in the soil break down, beneficial insects get killed and the fertility of the soil is reduced. By growing your own food, you can choose which pesticides and insecticides to use.

Effects on Other Plants

In order for some plants to thrive they need lots of nitrogen. Crops such as peas and beans help fix nitrogen in the soil which is why advocates of traditional crop rotation suggest you sow crops that *need* nitrogen in the same space as you grew *nitrogen fixing* plants the previous season. Unfortunately, some pesticides can interfere with nitrogen fixation resulting in reduced crop yields.

Did You Know?

**Potatoes are the most common source of vegetable waste.
Grow your own and harvest what you need as you need it!**

Effects on Bees

Pesticides have recently been blamed for contributing to colony collapse disorder. This can kill honeybees which are responsible for pollinating one third of the food we eat. The USDA estimate that farmers lose at least $200 million a year from reduced crop pollination. This is because pesticides applied to fields eliminate about a fifth of honeybee colonies in the US and harm an additional 15 per cent. You can choose to garden organically and *encourage* bees to your garden.

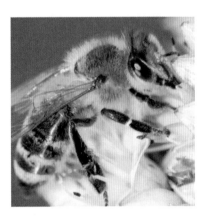

Effects on Animals

If wild animals (or indeed domestic ones) enter areas that have recently been sprayed with pesticides they can be harmed when they eat contaminated foods or pick up chemicals on their fur and feet which they then clean. Over a period of time, widespread use of pesticides can completely eliminate food sources that certain wild animals need. They either starve or have to relocate. If they relocate this upsets the ecosystem and food chain.

Effects on Birds

Several bird species have been killed either by an accumulation of pesticides in their tissues or loss of natural food such as earthworms or insects. In other cases, pesticides that come in granular form can be mistaken for food and eaten by birds which then die. By gardening at home, you can take full responsibility for the storage and use of any chosen pesticides.

Intensive Farming

Intensive farming means lots of food can be grown year after year in the same soil, which means you benefit from lower prices. The downside is that mechanical ploughing, chemical fertilizers and use of pesticides can increase soil erosion, destroy natural habitat, decrease soil fertility and contaminate the air and water supplies. By growing your own food, you can help support the environment.

More Choices

By growing food at home you have the ability to:

 Rotate crops.

 Use selective pesticides.

 Be conservative with water usage.

 Ensure fertilizers are used correctly.

 Attract beneficial insects and wildlife to reduce insecticide use.

 Use companion plants to reduce herbicide dependency.

 Employ organic, biodynamic or permaculture gardening.

Checklist

Remember to consider the following when troubleshooting:

Time: Keeping your garden free of pests, diseases and weeds takes time and commitment; how could you fit this into your weekly schedule?

Go organic: Are you going to grow organically? If so, you may want to consider finding information on companion planting and beneficial insects.

Prevention: Most pests, weeds and diseases can be controlled by a 'prevention rather than cure' approach to gardening.

Clearing: Keep your plot, no matter how big or small, free from decayed plants and other debris.

TLC: By taking care to raise healthy plants, you'll reduce the risks of pests and diseases.

Compost: Make sure you use good quality compost from a reputable source; good soil means good plants.

Pesticides: If you are going to use pesticides and herbicides, decide which would be best for you to use.

Damage: Familiarize yourself with different pest and disease damage so you can deal with any straight away.

Vegetables & Salads

Tender Vegetables

Tender vegetables include tomatoes, peppers and aubergines; Mediterranean plants that require a lot of sunlight and warmth and don't tolerate harsh conditions. These plants are often grown in greenhouses, but you can grow them against a sheltered wall or inside your home on large windowsills.

Tomatoes

Tomatoes are one of the most common vegetables to be grown in pots and it's easy to see why. They are particularly suited to container gardening; you can use individual pots, growbags, hanging baskets, window boxes or grow them indoors on a sunny windowsill. Use tumbling tomatoes for hanging baskets and window boxes.

Growing from Seed

Tomato seed is sown around March or April (early to mid-spring) indoors. Sow the seeds into trays and keep them on a windowsill. When they are sturdy enough to handle, put in slightly larger pots.

Once the plants are about 20 cm (8 in) tall they can be hardened off and planted outdoors. If you don't have any available space inside, sow them straight into their containers outdoors, but wait until the soil is warm and frosts have passed.

Position and Soil

Tomatoes need a lot of sun and fertile, well-drained soil. They are often grown in greenhouses because they like warmth; so

a south-facing wall is the ideal position for your pot, or you could use a south-facing windowsill and grow indoors in a large pot. Most tomatoes, apart from tumbling and compact varieties require support – a bamboo cane is ideal – with string tied loosely around the stems to keep them in place.

Care of Tomatoes

Tomatoes require regular and vigilant watering. They wilt easily and insufficient watering can lead to blossom end rot; a calcium deficiency. If you then over water the plants, the fruits can split or end up tasteless. Tomatoes are hungry plants which require high potash feed once the fruits start forming.

Pests and Diseases

The main pests to attack tomatoes are aphids and whitefly; although these are generally a problem for tomatoes grown in greenhouses. Conversely, tomatoes grown outdoors are more prone to potato blight, so keep a fungicide handy.

Varieties

'Gardeners Delight' are small, sweet fruits which retain a good 'bite' and are delicious eaten in salads. 'Sweet Million' will provide you with up to 50 tiny tomatoes per truss. Try 'Tumbling Tom' for hanging baskets or window boxes. 'Totem' grow 30 cm (12 in) high plants producing high yields of large cherry tomatoes which are perfect for indoors.

Did You Know?
Tomatoes are in fact a fruit, not a vegetable.

Peppers

Peppers include the large red, yellow, green and orange sweet peppers commonly seen in supermarkets, but they also include chillies. They are ideal in pots and do well if grown indoors on a south-facing windowsill or conservatory. It's not impossible to grow them outdoors, but they do need a warm, sheltered spot.

Growing from Seed

Pepper seed is sown around April (mid-spring) and the mature plants require rich compost. Sow seeds in seed trays on a windowsill indoors. When they have two or three leaves, put the plants in slightly larger pots. Once the plant's roots fill the pot (i.e. you can see them through the holes at the bottom of the pot), they can be hardened off and planted outdoors or put into a bigger pot inside. Peppers can also be grown in growbags. Before planting outside, ensure all risks of frost have passed.

Position and Soil

Peppers need a lot of sun, warm temperatures and rich compost which drains well. A south-facing wall or windowsill is the ideal position for your pot. Peppers do not always ripen on the plant except in hot climates; it's OK to pick them when green and let them change colour indoors. It's better to pick the peppers when green anyway because if you leave the first fruits to mature on the stems this will prevent the growth of further fruit.

Care of Peppers

Peppers require regular, light watering and they like frequent liquid feeding. It's good to keep peppers in a small pot until they go into their final container because restricting the roots encourages the plant to fruit. Stake your plants otherwise the stems can break when the fruits are growing.

Pests and Diseases

Peppers need humidity to help prevent the red spider mite, so if the weather is very hot and dry spray the plants with a water mister or place the pot in a tray of pebbles that you keep damp. Aphids can attack pepper plants; these can be sprayed off with water to which you have added a drop of detergent, or you can pick clusters of aphids off by hand. Blossom end rot can occur through irregular watering – this can be prevented with a careful watering routine.

Did You Know?

Contrary to popular belief, the seeds are NOT the hottest part of peppers. Where the seed is attached to the white membrane inside the pepper is the hottest part.

Varieties

Pretty much any variety of pepper will grow well in a large enough container. If you want to try something different, 'Lilac Bell' as the name suggests is a lilac-coloured variety; the fruits grow to around 10 cm (4 in). 'Apache' has a high yield of 4 cm (1.5 in) long fruits. For window boxes, try 'Redskin' which produces a crop of fruits around the same length.

Aubergines

Aubergines (eggplants), like peppers, are ideal in pots and do well if grown indoors on a south-facing windowsill or conservatory. They can be grown outdoors in a warm, sheltered spot but require a lengthy growing season.

Growing from Seed

Aubergine seeds are sown around April (mid-spring) and the plants require fertile soil. Sow seeds in seed trays on a windowsill indoors. When the plants have two leaves, they can be moved into larger pots. Alternatively plant seeds straight into the final growing place to minimize root disturbance. Once all risk of frost has passed, aubergine plants can be hardened off and planted outdoors. You can keep the soil warm in outdoor containers by using cloches.

Position and Soil

Aubergines need a lot of sun, warm temperatures and rich compost which drains well. A south-facing wall or windowsill is the ideal position for your pot. Pick the fruits regularly as they appear to keep the plant producing more fruit.

Care of Aubergines

Aubergines require regular, light watering and need feeding with an all-purpose fertilizer every 10 days once the fruits set. Stake plants otherwise the stems can break when the fruits are growing.

Pests and Diseases

Aubergines need humidity, so if the weather is very hot and dry spray the plants with a water mister or stand the pots in a tray of damp pebbles. If the plants get too dry they can be attacked by the red spider mite. Aphids can be picked off by hand or 'washed' off with a blast of water with a drop of detergent in it. If humidity gets *too* high, botrytis can occur, but this is less likely when you grow the plants outside. Aubergines prefer to be in a pot on their own, rather than sharing it with other plants.

Varieties

'Baby Belle' is a bushy, dwarf variety. 'Thai Yellow Egg' produces egg-sized, golden yellow fruits. 'Fairy Tale' is a compact growing variety which is great for containers. The fruits are early to mature, approximately 50 days from transplanting and are best harvested when about 10 cm (4 in) long.

Top Tip

For plants that don't like root disturbance, use toilet rolls as 'seed trays' and put the whole lot in a big pot when you're ready to transplant – the cardboard will rot down and the roots will remain undisturbed.

Beans and Sweetcorn

Beans and sweetcorn traditionally take up lots of room in the garden; runner beans, for example, grow tall and require a good rooting to stay firmly in the ground. With compact, dwarf varieties now available, you can grow certain varieties of beans and sweetcorn successfully in large containers.

Broad Beans

Broad beans (fava beans) can be grown in pots but it's not ideal as they prefer space. However they are worth trying, especially if you have raised beds, because they are the first of the beans to mature which means you can be enjoying them late spring. If you do decide to grow them, choose compact varieties.

Growing from Seed

Some broad bean seeds can be sown during October or November (mid–late autumn) for an early spring crop. Keep them warm with cloches or straw. Alternatively plant straight into large outdoor pots in February or March until the end of May for a continual supply.

Position and Soil

Broad beans like fertile, moisture-retentive soil. They can be over-wintered in all but the harshest climates where they will take around six to seven months to mature. When planted in the spring they can take just three to four months from sowing to harvest which makes them a nice, quick crop for beginners.

Care of Broad Beans

Broad beans are pretty easy-going crops and are not too fussy about soil condition. In very exposed areas, broad beans benefit from staking, but this is not generally needed. They need regular watering when the pods are swelling, but will tolerate a little neglect.

Pests and Diseases

Broad beans are prone to blackfly. This can be avoided by pinching out the growing tops as it is the smell of these that attracts blackfly.

Varieties

'The Sutton' is a compact variety for over-wintering that only reaches a height of 30–45 cm (12–18 in) making it suitable for containers and exposed areas.

Did you Know?

Broad beans are among the most ancient plants in cultivation and also among the easiest to grow.

Runner Beans and Dwarf Beans

Runner beans and dwarf beans are a great crop for beginners and they can be successfully grown in large pots and raised beds. Dwarf beans produce smaller plants around 30 cm (1 ft) tall, so these can be grown in window boxes, whereas runner bean plants grow too tall and need more space.

Growing from Seed

Runner bean and dwarf bean seeds can be sown straight into large pots outdoors, full of rich, moisture-retentive soil. Put two seeds side by side and take out the weaker looking seedling, leaving the stronger plant.

Position and Soil

Runner beans grow tall, so ensure you use a large, heavy pot with a wide base to prevent plants falling over or use a raised bed. If the temperature rises too high, runner beans will not set seed, so you can keep them in a cooler place if you live in a hot climate. Dwarf beans grow bushier and compact so if your plot is smaller or you live in an area which is exposed to winds, opt for dwarf beans.

Care of Beans

Beans need lots of water when the flowers set to ensure the beans grow properly. Tall beans need some canes to grow up otherwise they will fall over. Pick both runner and dwarf beans every other day or so during the harvest season to get a continual crop because once one pod matures on the plant it will stop producing new pods. As beans like lots of water, it is important to keep a check on weeds.

Pests and Diseases

Slugs love runner bean seedlings. You can protect against these with barriers or traps. If you have the room, have a few seedlings on standby to replace ones that get eaten!

Varieties

'Hestia' is a perfect runner bean for pots as it is a dwarf plant. Hestia is early to crop and provides a good yield but it grows like a bush so doesn't need staking. For dwarf beans, try 'Delinel' which is a heavy-cropping, stringless bean.

Top Tip

Beans need a lot of water, so why not syphon off your bathwater to use in your containers?

Baby Sweetcorn

Although not ideal for pots, mini sweetcorn can be grown in large tubs or deep raised beds.

Growing from Seed

Sweetcorn needs to be grown in blocks rather than rows to pollinate successfully. Sow the seeds directly into a large rectangular container from April to June (mid-spring–early summer). Once the plants are established and temperatures warm up, you'll be amazed how fast these plants grow.

Position and Soil

Even mini sweetcorn grow tall, so you'll need to put them in a sheltered area and plant in a deep, heavy container to prevent them being blown over. Despite being tall plants, they don't require staking, however be aware they may prevent sun reaching other plants, so bear this in mind when choosing where to plant them. They need a position in full sun, a long warm summer and require rich soil; a sheltered suntrap in your plot is ideal.

Care of Sweetcorn

Sweetcorn need heat to germinate and don't like being moved, so it's better to plant them late in the season when the soil is warm and all risk of frost has passed. You can pop the seeds in biodegradable pots if you want to start them off earlier indoors. The plants require a lot of water to swell the cobs and it's important the soil doesn't dry out between watering. They are ready for harvest when the silks turn brown, although if you are growing a mini variety such as 'Mini Pop' they should be picked when the tassels just start to appear.

Pests and Diseases

Mice love sweetcorn, but these are usually less problematic with container gardening. The most likely cause of a failed crop is lack of pollination. This can be due to over-dry soil or cool climate. You can obviously take care of ensuring the plants have enough water, but you need to choose the sowing time wisely.

Varieties

'Mini Pop' has been especially bred to produce mini corn. Pick them before the tassels appear and you should get three to five cobs per plant which are perfect for stir fries and salads.

Top Tip

The sugar in sweetcorn begins to turn to starch as soon as it is removed from the plant so make sure you cut it when you are ready to boil and eat it.

Root Vegetables

Traditionally grown in long rows in an allotment, you might be surprised to learn that most root vegetables also grow well in containers. You can buy baby beetroot and short-rooted carrots while radishes are also a good choice for containers. This section covers beetroot, carrots, radishes, mini parsnips and potatoes.

Beetroot

Mini beetroot (mini beet) are ideal for containers and you can harvest the leaves to use like spinach.

Growing from Seed

Beetroot are best sown directly into the container mid spring and can be sown under cover from late winter to early spring. They can be ready in as little as 10 weeks. Once the seedlings come through, thin them out to give room to grow.

Position and Soil

Beetroot need light, free-draining soil and cool but sunny conditions which means they are not suitable for hotter climates. They will grow well in pots, raised beds and window boxes.

Care of Beetroot

Beetroot need regular water during the growing season otherwise they become hard and woody but they are pretty resilient and can be left to their own devices. Harvest when small and their shoulders poke out of the soil and cook in a number of ways – they can be roasted, boiled, made into soup or eaten raw.

Pests and Diseases

Beetroot are pretty much trouble free. However, if the weather becomes too hot they can bolt (grow too quickly) easily.

Varieties

'Solo' is an ideal baby beetroot that produces high-quality globes without the need for thinning. 'Detroit 2 Tardel' is perfect if you want to pickle your beetroot. 'Pablo' stores well without going woody and is a good choice for 'baby beet' production. The young leaves can be used like spinach.

Carrots

Carrots are the perfect crop for containers because not all people have the right soil for a successful crop.

Top Tip

Instead of thinning out beetroot seedlings as you would in an open plot, you can leave them closer together in a pot to grow smaller globes.

Growing from Seed

Carrots need to be sown as thinly as possible early spring into warm, damp soil. If the soil is not warm enough, it's better to wait.

Position and Soil

Prepare a light, sandy soil in your container to ensure the best harvest; carrots will not grow well in heavy soils. Try one third horticultural sand, one third compost and one third topsoil.

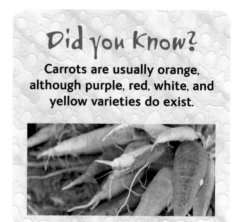

Did you know?

Carrots are usually orange, although purple, red, white, and yellow varieties do exist.

Care of Carrots

Carrot seedlings need careful thinning out. If at all possible, sow them thinly to begin with to prevent having to thin them at a later stage; this will reduce the risk of carrot fly. The established plants need minimal watering and sudden watering can cause the roots to fork. The carrots are ready when their shoulders poke out of the soil, but it's better to leave them in there until you are ready to eat them. Just pull out one or two for your meal and leave the rest in the pot until needed.

Pests and Diseases

The worst carrot pests are carrot fly. These lay eggs and the maggots burrow into the soil where they eat into and damage the roots. The carrot fly is attracted to the scent which is given off when the leaves are disturbed or bruised during thinning out. This is why it is better to sow thinly and not have to thin out the crop. However, growing in containers is advantageous as the carrot fly cannot fly very high, so if your container is tall enough the fly won't be able to reach your crop! Alternatively, cover with horticultural fleece.

Varieties

Most varieties are suitable for containers as long as the container is deep enough for the root to fully form. Round or stump-rooted carrots are ideal for more shallow pots and window boxes.

'Paris Market Atlas' is an early carrot with almost round roots which is ideal for shallow containers. 'Amsterdam Forcing' has slim blunt-ended roots and is a heavy yielder suitable for baby carrots in a deeper container.

Parsnips

Parsnips take a long time to mature so you should only grow them if you really have the space for them or you love them so much it's worth the trouble.

Growing from Seed

Sow parsnip seed in situ into warmed soil from early spring. You can use cloches to help keep the soil warm. Make sure the container is deep enough for the roots to push down and don't try and grow full-sized varieties – opt for 'mini' versions.

Position and Soil

Parsnips like sandy soil, so mix compost with sand to improve the drainage; around 70 per cent multi-purpose compost with 30 per cent horticultural sand is ideal. You'll need to allow around 16 cm (6 in) between each seedling when it comes through, so thin them out carefully.

Care of Parsnips

Once the seedlings are established, the hardest work has been done as germination is usually the most difficult part of growing parsnips. Parsnips need to be watered during dry spells to make sure the roots develop well. At the beginning of autumn, the foliage will die down and you can gently loosen the soil around the crop and pull it up, although you only need to pull up parsnips when you want to eat them because they will happily sit in the ground. Some people swear that a frost improves the flavour.

Pests and Diseases

Parsnips suffer from carrot fly which you can prevent by covering your crop in horticultural fleece. Canker is the most serious parsnip disease which looks like dark patches on the shoulders of the carrots which then go soft and rotten. Sometimes waiting until later in the year before sowing can help.

Varieties

'Javelin' can be sown 8 cm (3 in) apart for mini parsnips with an excellent flavour. 'Lancer' can be sown close together for small parsnips too.

Potatoes

Potatoes are one of the simplest and most exciting crops to grow. There is nothing like rooting through a container to find new potatoes, even for experienced gardeners!

Growing from Seed

Purchase potato sets from a reputable nursery and 'chit' them by putting them in a shallow tray (old egg boxes are ideal) with the eyes facing upwards in a cool, frost free, light place a couple of weeks before you intend to plant them. Take your chitted potatoes in early spring and push them into your prepared container, with the eyes facing upwards, about an inch below the surface.

Position and Soil

Potatoes will grow virtually anywhere in most types of soil. You can use a variety of large containers; there are specialized potato planters or you could use a stack of tyres, an old dustbin or even a large, strong bag such as a builders' merchant bag.

Care of Potatoes

Potatoes need 'earthing up' two or three times as they grow which means covering the plants with more soil. This prevents potatoes turning green and increases the crop. Keep lightly watered and increase the watering slightly when flowers appear on the haulms. Once the flowers start to die, you can gently fork through the soil with a trowel or your hands to find your treasures. Early potatoes are ready around three months after planting.

Pests and Diseases

Blight can affect potatoes, but if you stick to 'early' varieties, rather than maincrop it shouldn't be a problem.

Varieties

Most 'earlies' are suitable for containers as long as the container is big enough. 'Rocket' and 'Vales Emerald' are good, hardy varieties that produce a decent-sized harvest.

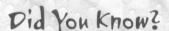

Did You Know?

The average person eats 500 medium-sized potatoes in a year.

Radish

Radishes are the ideal crop for beginners because they grow quickly and will thrive in virtually any container, however shallow. Children love to grow radishes because the results are so quick; around six weeks from sowing to harvest.

Growing from Seed

Radish seeds are sown in situ in any free-draining soil from February to August (late winter to late summer); although seeds sown early will need protecting with cloches to ensure germination. Sow them in moist, warm soil.

Position and Soil

Radishes will tolerate some shade, in fact, having them in an exposed sunny spot can cause them to bolt; this makes them perfect for planting between other crops which can provide dappled shade from the midday sun. They are the ideal crop for successive sowing and if you plant them less than 2.5 cm (1 in) apart you will get a small, tender crop.

Care of Radishes

Radishes need regular watering to produce the best crop; if you don't keep them moist enough they can get woody. Harvest the radishes when small otherwise they can get tough and very hot! They do not last well in the ground, so pull them up as soon as they are ready. They can take as little as six weeks from sowing to harvest.

Pests and Diseases

Radishes are not really bothered by pests except the flea beetle which make holes in the leaves. This can be prevented with the use of horticultural fleece.

Varieties

'Scarlet Globe' is a popular variety with quick-growing, scarlet roots. 'Jolly Speedy' has a mild flavour and is quick to reach maturity.

Did You Know?

Although you might be used to small red globes bought in supermarkets, radishes can be white, pink, black, pointed or cylindrical.

Squash

Some squash, such as pumpkins are so big both in size and feeding requirements that they are not really suitable for container gardening, however others, such as courgettes are better because you don't end up with marrows so quickly! In this section you'll learn how to grow courgettes, cucumber and mini squash.

Courgettes

Even though courgettes (zucchini) can grow huge in open soil, they do well in large containers, raised beds and growbags. They are very easy to grow and great for beginners.

Growing from Seed

Courgette seeds can be sown indoors and transplanted later or placed in situ once the ground and air are warm from April to early June (mid-spring to early summer).

Position and Soil

Courgettes like rich soil and sun. Ideally, you would plant them in moisture-retentive compost.

Care of Courgettes

Courgettes like to be kept moist and will pretty much take care of themselves. Make sure you water regularly otherwise you can end up with deformed fruits. The most important thing is to give them enough space – make sure your container is large enough and only put one plant per pot. Courgettes are hungry feeders, so use a fertilizer when the fruits are swelling. The harvesting season is short but prolific; make sure you have some favourite recipes on hand because once your courgettes ripen you'll be getting several a week. You may need to keep fruits up off the soil when they are forming to stop them rotting, although this is usually more of a problem on open soil. Harvest the small fruits regularly; if you leave a courgette to turn into a marrow it will prevent other fruits being formed.

Pests and Diseases

Courgettes can suffer from powdery mildew which looks like a grey fuzz on their leaves. To prevent this keep the soil moist and if the problem gets too bad use a fungicide. Slugs like the seedlings so either protect them with barriers or traps or grow the seeds indoors and transplant the courgette plants once they are established.

Top Tip

Courgettes do not freeze well, but if you make them into soup or ratatouille first this will help you deal with a glut.

Varieties

'Eight Ball' gives high yields of small, dark green ball-shaped fruits on compact plants. 'Patriot' is early fruiting and is extremely prolific.

Cucumber

You can successfully grow cucumbers in large containers and they are, in fact, easier to grow outdoors than in a greenhouse.

Growing from Seed

Once the weather is warm enough, cucumber seeds can be sown outdoors, in situ, from mid to late spring. If necessary, use a cloche over the seeds to keep the soil warm. Alternatively sow in small pots indoors and transplant to larger, outdoor containers once the plants are established.

Position and Soil

Cucumbers like rich soil and sun and need warmth to germinate. Ideally, you would plant them in moisture-retentive compost. When growing cucumbers in a container, it's good to give them a stick to climb up.

Care of Cucumbers

Cucumbers like to be kept moist and warm in order to grow successfully. Once the fruit is forming, it is essential to water regularly. Cucumbers are hungry and may require feeding as the fruits form with fertilizer. Harvest when small to keep the plant producing new fruit.

Pests and Diseases

Slugs like the young plants, so protect them with barriers or traps. Cucumbers can suffer from powdery mildew – keep a fungicide on hand to deal with this.

Varieties

'La Diva' produces mini cucumbers about 15 cm (6 in) long with good disease-resistance properties. 'Hana' can be grown indoors on a large windowsill. It is early cropping and produces prolific short fruits. 'Iznik' produces high yields of 10–12 cm (4 in) fruits which grow well in containers, growbags or in a conservatory.

Did You Know?

'Cool as a cucumber'? The inner temperature of a cucumber can be up to 20 degrees cooler than the outside air!

Squash

There are two main types of squash – summer and winter. Obviously you wouldn't try to grow a huge pumpkin in a container, but some of the smaller squashes, such as acorn or patty pan, can grow well in large pots and raised beds.

Acorn squashes are of the 'winter' type.

Growing from Seed

Once the weather is warm enough, squash seeds can be sown outdoors, in situ. If you need to, use a cloche over the seed to keep the soil warm. Sow two seeds and thin the weaker one out to leave the stronger plant. Alternatively sow in small pots indoors, harden off and transplant to larger, outdoor containers once the plants are established and all risk of frost has passed.

Position and Soil

Squashes like rich soil, a sunny spot and need warmth to germinate. They will grow quite happily on a compost heap, so ensure your container is filled with rich soil.

Care of Squashes

Squashes require a lot of water during the growing season to swell the fruits, but once their leaves have spread they provide their own soil cover to help prevent evaporation. They also need feeding with an all-purpose fertilizer. If the temperature suddenly drops you will need to protect your young plants with cloches. If you get a lot of fruit on one vine, remove some of them to prevent them competing for food; three or four squashes per plant is ideal. Pick squashes when the fruits are young and tender.

Pests and Diseases

Slugs like the young plants and tender fruits, so protect them with barriers or traps. Squashes can suffer from powdery mildew; keep a fungicide on hand to deal with this and make sure the soil is kept moist to avoid it happening. To prevent the fruits rotting, keep them off the soil with an old tile, brick or a mound of hay.

Varieties

For summer squash, try 'Lunar Eclipse', a patty pan shaped variety which matures quickly. For winter squash 'Honey Bear' is ideal for containers. They have a sweet flesh and the plants are no larger than a courgette plant.

Onion Family

Some of the smaller onion family such as garlic and chives are ideal for containers. You can buy mini leeks and shallots or spring onions can be grown in small containers because they are shallow rooting. In this section you'll discover how to grow garlic, mini leeks, shallots and spring onions.

Garlic

Garlic is a great crop for beginners and it's amazing to see how one individual clove develops into an entire bulb!

Growing from Seed

You need to buy garlic from a garden centre and you can plant it directly into your container during autumn for an early summer harvest. Break the bulb into individual cloves, but don't remove the papery skin. Push each clove down into the soil until the tip is an inch below the soil and space them 10 cm (4 in) apart.

Garlic is a nice crop for children to take care of because it can be grown in very small pots. You can plant one clove in a 13 cm x 5 cm (5 x 2 in) pot filled with potting compost.

Position and Soil

Garlic likes free-draining soil and needs a sunny site, so make sure it is not sheltered by other, taller plants. Keep it in containers close to your house during autumn to keep it warm.

Care of garlic

Garlic is nice and easy to take care of. As long as the pot doesn't become waterlogged and you keep weeds away your garlic should grow well. Water if the soil becomes too dry otherwise leave it to take care of itself. Garlic is ready when the leaves begin to shrivel and turn yellowy brown. Pull up the bulbs, gently loosening the soil around each one with a trowel, and leave to dry in the sun or hang them up and allow the air to circulate. When the skin turns papery, the garlic is ready to be used.

Pests and Diseases

Garlic pretty much takes care of itself although it can rot if conditions are too wet or the soil does not drain well.

Varieties

'Solent Wight' is a popular choice that can be harvested in July. 'Jolimont' is a great-tasting garlic that stores well.

Did you know?
Evidence of garlic has been found in caves inhabited more than 10,000 years ago.

Leeks

Traditionally leeks take up a lot of space for a long time in the vegetable plot. However, they can be grown in large pots and raised beds to be harvested when small. They are worth growing because they are available during winter when many other crops are over.

Growing from Seed

Leek seeds are sown indoors mid winter, ready for planting out mid spring, so they are not ideal for those with limited space. When the plants are as thick as a pencil and the soil has warmed in your containers you can transplant them into large, deep containers. Leeks are unusual in that, instead of filling the prepared hole with soil once the leek is planted, you fill it with water. The easiest way to grow mini leeks, however, is to plant them directly into long containers such as deep window boxes and thin seedlings to around 1 cm (½ in) as they emerge.

> ### Did You Know?
> To get a nice white stem, you'll have to earth up your leeks as they grow. The sun turns the stalks green.

Position and Soil

Leeks are fairly fuss-free; they like sun and loamy soil but will tolerate many conditions.

Care of Leeks

Once they are growing well, leeks pretty much take care of themselves. As long as you keep weeds away and water during very dry spells, leeks don't need much attention. You can leave leeks in your containers, even throughout the winter, until you want to eat them.

Pests and Diseases

The most common problem with leeks is rust which is a fungus. To help prevent rust, keep weeds at bay and don't sow the leeks too thickly together as this creates humidity for the fungal spores to germinate. Leeks can suffer from onion fly, where tunnelling maggots can rot the crop. Use horticultural fleece to prevent this.

Varieties

'Jolant' is a mild-flavoured baby leek. You can either plant one or two in a large pot or plant more, closer together, for baby vegetables. 'Tornado' is good for baby leeks and can tolerate a very cold climate.

Shallots – good for pots!

Shallots and Onions

It's not worth growing large onions in containers, but shallots and spring onions (scallions) work well. Shallots are sweeter and milder than onions without any acidity, while spring onions are ideal for adding to salads or stir fries.

Growing from Seed

Shallots are best grown from sets in moisture-retentive soil. Push individual shallots into a prepared containers from the end of winter through the spring and they'll be ready to harvest in around four months. Push them down until just the tip shows above the soil, either in individual pots or 15 cm (6 in) apart in a large container or raised bed.

You can plant spring onion seeds in the autumn ready for an early spring harvest although you may need to protect with cloches in severe weather. Sow thinly, around 2.5 cm (1 in) apart in pre-watered shallow drills, and cover with a little more soil.

Spring onions are good in salads and stir fries.

Position and Soil

Shallots and spring onions need free-draining but moisture-retentive soil that does not become waterlogged – this is much easier to manage in containers than in the ground.

Care of Shallots and Spring Onions

Keep weeds from competing for water and nutrients and make sure the shallots never get too wet. When the foliage starts to turn yellow, your shallots are ready to harvest. Loosen the soil around the bulbs with a trowel then hang them up to dry in the sunshine or an airy place. Keep spring onion seedlings moist until established. There is no need to thin them, just pull when the onions are young and thin. You can sow little and often for a continuous supply throughout the summer.

Pests and Diseases

The most common problem with the onion family is onion fly. You can use horticultural fleece to prevent damage. Onions can also suffer from mildew or mould, but only if they get too wet.

Varieties

'White Lisbon' is the most popular spring onion which is quick cropping and very hardy. 'Ramrod' is a winter hardy spring onion, so can be sown in autumn. 'Jermor ' is the best variety of shallot for cooking and 'Picasso' is highly resistant to bolting and perfect for pickling.

Top Tip

To avoid eye irritation when preparing onions, cut them under running water or submerged in a basin of water.

Leafy Crops and Salad

Leafy crops such as spinach and chard can take up a lot of room in a traditional plot. However, planted close together and confined in containers they make a great edible crop for pots of all sizes. You can harvest the leaves when they are small and use in salads. Kale is the only cabbage plant you are likely to grow, and if you only have one container and are completely new to gardening then salad leaves are the perfect crop for you!

Chard is hardier than spinach.

Harvest spinach early to get baby leaves.

Chard and Spinach

Chard – also known as Swiss chard – is a great crop to grow because it lasts through the winter, grows more the more you cut it and does well in containers. It's also a very pretty crop with its multi-coloured varieties. Spinach is also a great container crop; it needs slightly more care than chard because it is frost-tender and doesn't like to get too dry, but it grows well in most climates.

Growing from Seed

Chard seeds can be planted in either autumn or spring in situ. Thin seedlings when they are about 10 cm (4 in) tall. Spinach can be sown between April and September (mid-spring and late summer) but it may not germinate in very hot weather. Sow spinach quite densely and harvest when the leaves are small for a baby crop.

Position and Soil

Chard and spinach like fertile, well-drained soil and thrive in cool climates. You can grow both crops in the shade of other plants and they are perfect choices if your plot is in partial shade.

Care of Spinach and Chard

If chard or spinach get too dry they will bolt, so water regularly during dry, hot spells. When you cut mature chard leaves, more will grow in their place, so it's a lovely crop for children to grow.

Rainbow chard is dazzling.

Choose perpetual spinach and plant in succession so you can treat it like a cut-and-come-again crop. Spinach is more prone to sulking if it gets too dry, whereas chard is more forgiving and better for novice gardeners, children or people without a lot of time. Both crops will be ready to eat two to three months after sowing.

Pests and Diseases

The biggest problem with chard and spinach is that slugs love the plants as much as you do. Protect your crop with barriers or traps. In dry conditions, spinach can develop powdery mildew; prevent this with careful watering.

Varieties

For spinach, 'Nagano' is fast maturing and high yielding, which is ideal for baby leaf, and resistant to downy mildew. For a stunning colour try 'Rhubarb' chard. As the name suggests, the stems are a beautiful deep crimson colour.

Did You Know?

Medieval artists extracted green pigment from spinach to use as an ink or paint.

Kale

There is really only one member of the cabbage family you would grow in containers, and that is kale. Kale is a great contender for pots and makes a useful vegetable for harvesting throughout the winter when other crops are unavailable. It is simple to grow and ideal for beginners as it will tolerate many different soils and conditions. It will even grow in part shade and improves its taste during cold weather.

Growing from Seed

Kale seeds can be sown straight into outdoor pots during late spring in any type of well-drained soil, although nitrogen rich is best. Sow thinly at a depth of approx 1 cm (½ in). If you decide to sow indoors and move them, plant out when approx 12 cm (5 in) high in a 50 cm (20 in) pot. Harvest from autumn onwards.

Position and Soil

Kale is not a particularly fussy plant; as long as it is given enough water and not choked by weeds it will flourish in most conditions and soils. It can even tolerate a bit of neglect. The only thing that might bother kale plants is too much heat so keep them sheltered from too much sun.

Care of Kale

Kale, like most plants, requires regular, light watering but will manage for a couple of days without. If the containers are in an exposed place, kale will require short stakes to prevent breakages. Once the leaves are large enough to harvest, cut them with a sharp knife and leave the rest of the plant in the soil to produce new leaves.

Pests and Diseases

Kale is one of the most hardy plants and only gets bothered by the cabbage white. The butterflies lay their eggs on kale leaves which hatch into hungry caterpillars that eat the leaves at an alarming rate. Prevent eggs being laid by using horticultural fleece.

Varieties

'Red Russian Kale' produces green leaves on purple stems and can be eaten raw in salads or stir fried. 'Dwarf Green Curled' is a popular choice for containers.

Top Tip

Kale is the perfect crop for novice gardeners because it is so hardy.

Salad Leaves

Salad leaves are a wonderful crop for growing at home in containers. They have shallow roots so are ideal for window boxes, small containers and growbags. Choosing salad leaves is simple with many 'mixed leaves' varieties available. You can choose hot and peppery ones or milder mixes to suit your own taste.

Growing from Seed

Seeds are scattered over warm compost in situ and covered lightly with more compost. For best results sow a few seeds in succession, every three weeks or so, for a continual harvest; otherwise you might end up with a large crop that gets woody before you can eat it. You can sow salad leaves from early spring to early autumn, right up until you get frost, and you'll be able to pick fresh salad virtually all year round.

Position and Soil

Salad leaves don't like intense sun and heat, so are perfect if you don't have a south-facing plot. You can plant them in window boxes outside your kitchen window or they will tolerate a little dappled shade from taller plants outside.

Care of Salad Leaves

Salad leaves, especially the cut-and-come-again varieties, are pretty easy to maintain. They grow quickly, which means they must be harvested quickly too, otherwise they soon go past their best. In most cases you can snip off just the leaves you want for your meal and more will grow in their place. Keep salad leaves well watered, but don't let them stand in water.

Pests and Diseases

The worst pest you will encounter with salad leaves is slugs who love the tender shoots as much as you do. Put traps or barriers around plants to protect them or sow a few 'sacrificial' lettuces around the edge of your salad for the slugs to eat. Alternatively use slug pellets.

Varieties

It's impossible to list all the salad leaves here, so it's worth taking time to browse your local garden centre to see what's on offer. Rocket and mizuna are spicy and peppery, while corn salad and little gem lettuces are mild. You can find mixes such as 'Italian Salad Mix', 'Spicy Oriental Leaves' or buy individual packets of the leaves you enjoy to make your own mixes.

Checklist

A reminder of what to consider when growing vegetables:

☑ **Sun**: Do you have a sunny conservatory to grow plants in? Try sun lovers such as tomatoes, aubergines and peppers.

☑ **Hanging baskets**: Do you only have room for hanging baskets? Tumbling tomatoes were designed for your plot!

☑ **Window boxes**: If you are only using window boxes you could grow compact bush dwarf beans, short-stumped carrots, mini beetroot, spring onions or radishes.

☑ **Raised beds**: If you have room for raised beds, you could grow any of the foods listed in this chapter.

☑ **Growbags**: Tomatoes, courgettes or peppers are best in growbags.

☑ **Shade**: Is your plot in partial shade? Try growing root crops.

☑ **Keep it simple**: Are you a complete novice? Some of the easiest crops to grow are potatoes, radishes and tomatoes.

☑ **Young gardeners**: Do your children want to take care of their own food? Potatoes and radishes are the easiest for them to nurture.

☑ **Go organic**: Are you growing organically? Plant carrots and spring onions close to one another to deter the carrot fly.

☑ **Family food**: Have you taken note of your family's favourite foods before choosing which vegetables to grow?

Fruit, Herbs
& Edible
Flowers

Fruit Trees

You could be forgiven for thinking fruit trees are only for people with huge gardens or orchards. Fortunately nothing could be further from the truth! Some fruits, such as figs thrive *better* in pots and there are lots of varieties of fruits suitable for all sorts of containers. You can even grow apple trees in containers, once you know which type you are looking for.

Which Trees Work Best?

You obviously can't plant a standard apple or plum tree in a container. You need to look for something called 'rootstock'. A rootstock is the stump of a plant with a healthy root system onto which a cutting (scion) from another plant is grafted. Each rootstock has different properties, including drought resistance, fruit size or final growth size so you can get the same scion grafted onto different rootstocks, which means you can get the perfect plant for your growing space.

Multi-variety

The beauty of rootstocks is that you can graft several different scions onto one rootstock and end up with an apple tree that provides you with three different apple varieties!

A six-week-old apple seedling.

Apple Trees

Although it is possible to grow apple trees in containers you need to choose the right sort. You need to look for one grown on a dwarfing rootstock such as M27 (which reaches six foot when full grown) or M9 (which reaches eight foot). Most apples need other apple trees to pollinate them, so you need to check this and either buy two or three. If you don't have room for more than one apple tree, buy a self-fertilizing variety.

Suitable Containers

For fruit trees you mustn't skimp on the container you choose. Buy the biggest you can afford such as a half barrel. Ensure the container has drainage holes at the bottom and put a layer of broken crocks in the bottom before filling with soil. Some people use old dustbins to plant apple trees in.

Soil and Planting

Apple trees need fertile, moisture-retentive soil that is well draining. Apple trees are traditionally planted during the autumn when the tree is dormant. This gives it the winter to settle into its new position. Apple trees like a sunny site.

Did You Know?

Apple varieties range in size from a little larger than a cherry to as large as a grapefruit.

Care of Apple Trees

Apple trees need regular watering so the container soil never dries out, especially during their first year. Feed the soil once a month to keep the tree healthy. During early spring, remove the top few inches of compost and replace with fresh compost to feed your tree. You may need to water your tree twice a week during the summer.

Pruning

When you buy dwarfing rootstocks, you'll notice that some require pruning and others don't – take this into account when making your final decision and choose one to suit your needs.

Varieties

Perfect for the small container garden are trees that have had two or three different varieties grafted on to the same rootstock. This way you can enjoy a few varieties of apple with only one tree.

Pests and Diseases

Look out for canker, mildew, rust and scab. Once the fruit have ripened wasps and birds are attracted to them; so make sure you get to the fruit before they do.

Harvest

It will take two or three years before you eat an apple from your tree. It's simple to test if an apple is ready to be picked; if you hold the apple in the palm of your hand and twist it once or twice, it will fall away easily when ready. Depending on the variety some apples need eating quickly, whereas others will store well.

Blueberry and Cranberry Plants

Blueberries and cranberries are particularly suitable for containers because they require the type of soil rarely found in gardens. Both are compact plants and are great fun for novices to grow.

Suitable Containers

Blueberries and cranberries need fairly large containers – 45 cm (18 in) should do the trick. You may get away with growing cranberries in a hanging basket or window box if you can manage to keep the compost moist enough.

Soil

Blueberries and cranberries need moist, acidic soil, so you will need to buy ericaceous compost from a garden centre. Blueberries like a very coarse texture compost, so mix ericaceous compost with wood chip such as conifer chippings.

'Pilgrim' is a good tumbling variety of cranberry.

Care and Position

Both fruits need to be watered with rain water to prevent the pH of the soil being altered, so only plant them if you have a way of gathering rain water, such as a small barrel. Unless you have a tiny pot try to have more than one blueberry plant to allow them to cross-pollinate and ensure a better crop. Both blueberries and cranberries like full sun in a sheltered spot; against a south-facing wall is ideal but they will tolerate partial shade if necessary. Feed the plants every month during the growing season.

Pruning

Blueberries fruit on two-year-old wood. If your plant has woody branches with no fruit buds on it, cut it out. The harder you prune blueberries the better fruit you will get.

Did You Know?

North America produces nearly 90 per cent of the world's blueberries.

Varieties

'Sunshine Blue' is a very reliable blueberry and is bushy and compact, reaching about 3ft tall. 'Top Hat' is a great blueberry for containers because it is a dwarf variety. The mature bush reaches a maximum height and spread of just 41–46 cm (16–24 in) yet it produces a heavy crop. 'Pilgrim' is a variety of cranberry that can be planted to tumble from the sides of a hanging basket. 'Early Black' is reported to be one of the easiest cranberries to grow.

Pests and Diseases

Blueberries and cranberries are pretty trouble free when it comes to pests and diseases; just be aware that once the fruit is ripened, you may need to protect it from birds.

'Sunshine Blue' is a reliable choice of blueberry.

Harvest

During late summer the fruits swell and reach their wonderful dark colours. Pick the berries before the frost comes and freeze or use fresh. Cranberries can be made into cranberry jelly ready for Christmas and blueberries make a delicious addition to muffins.

Citrus Fruit

Oranges, lemons and limes can be grown successfully in containers as long as they get enough heat and sunshine during the summer and can be kept frost free during the winter. For this reason, some people grow them in conservatories or on sunny windowsills. If you want to move patio-grown fruits indoors during the winter you'll need to make sure you can move the pot, either by choosing one on wheels or using a sack truck.

Solent Wight ⎤ garlic
Jolimont   ⎦

White Lisbon ⎤ spring
Ramrod   ⎦ onion

.hic up

19 x 14 x 5 high

22 x 17 x 6

25 x 19 x 8

Picture
14" wide 29½" tall 1" deep.

Gardeners Delight
Sweet Million
Tumbling Tom
Totem only grows 12"

⎤ Tom
⎦ ato

Jolly Speedy radish
Scarlet Globe radish
La Diva cucumber - 6" long

Table
40cm high 80cm diameter

Suitable Containers

Citrus trees need to be potted on every year as the plant grows, so bear this in mind when planning your garden. Select a 2 ft (60 cm) terracotta pot for new citrus plants. Make sure the container has drainage holes and use a layer of crocks in the bottom. You can even add a layer of sand on top before filling the container with soil because well-drained soil is an essential requirement for the citrus family.

Soil

Citrus fruit require well-drained, fertile soil.

Top Tip

Rub your hands with fresh lemon to remove odours such as fish and onion.

Care and Position

Citrus fruits must not get waterlogged, so good drainage and careful watering is essential. Little and often is the key, rather than a good soaking. Feed citrus plants once a month during the growing season.

Varieties

For lemons try 'Meyer', which is a cross between a lemon and a mandarin and produces compact, round fruits on trees that are more hardy than other lemon trees. For oranges, try 'Calamondin'; these grow to approx 45 cm (18 in), are ideal for novices and are nearly always flowering and fruiting which makes them very ornamental. For lime trees a 'Tahiti' bush is excellent for growing in a pot in a conservatory.

'Calamondin' oranges are a good choice for novices.

Pests and Diseases

Red spider mite can affect citrus fruits that are grown indoors; increasing humidity will prevent this. Outdoor plants can suffer from root rot which is why you must ensure the soil is well drained. Citrus fruits suffer from aphids which should be easily spotted and picked off before they become a problem.

Figs

Figs are perfect for containers and even if you have a huge garden where space is not a problem, figs are better when contained in a pot because the roots are built to survive and will take over!

Suitable Containers

Choose a strong container, not one made of plastic. Concrete or brick is ideal. Limit the container to 60 cm (2 ft) so the plant produces fruit instead of lots of leaves.

Soil

Figs don't need particularly high quality compost; a multi-purpose compost is fine.

Care and Position

Figs need a lot of sunlight and heat so it's best to position them against a south-facing wall; the hotter the place, the happier they are. Figs need regular watering and feeding. If the compost dries out the plant will drop all its fruit, so only keep a fig if you can maintain a regular watering routine.

Varieties

If you are in a particularly cold climate, 'Violetta' can withstand temperatures of minus 20 degrees for a few days. 'Brown Turkey' crops heavily and is one of the most widely grown and reliable varieties.

Pests and Diseases

Birds and wasps are fond of figs, so use netting when the fruit has set.

Harvest

Figs do not ripen once picked, so make sure they are fully ripe before harvesting. When they are ready, they will pull away from the plant easily. Either eat them fresh, store in the refrigerator for a couple of days or freeze until you have enough to make jam.

'Brown Turkey' figs provide a good yield.

Did You Know?

The fig is one of the earliest fruits to be stored by man.

Pears

Like apples you will need to make sure a pear tree intended for a container is growing on a dwarfing rootstock. 'Quince C' rootstock will grow trees up to 2.4 m (8 ft) which is reasonable to take care of in a large container.

Container and Soil

Choose the largest container available to you, half barrels are ideal. Make sure it is at least 60 cm (24 in) deep. Pears need fertile, moisture-retentive soil that is well draining. You can try a mix of equal quantities of compost, well-rotted manure and top soil.

Care and position

Pears like a sunny, sheltered position and do not tolerate wind; against a south-facing wall is ideal. You'll need two pear trees to fertilize one another unless you buy a self-fertile variety. Pear trees ideally need watering every day in the summer when contained in pots to keep them healthy and they need regular feeding once a month during the growing season. During late autumn, take off the top few inches of compost and replace with new.

Pruning

Like apple trees, pears need pruning to remove dead wood.

Harvesting

You should pick pears when they are still hard and allow them to ripen at room temperature off the tree. Once they are ripe, pears do not store particularly well, so eat them fresh, bake into pies and freeze or preserve in syrup.

Varieties

'Terrace Pearl' is a dwarf pear tree that reaches a maximum height of approximately 1.2–1.5 m (4–5 ft). It is heavy cropping and can be grown in a container on the patio. It requires little pruning.

Top Tip

Harvest pears before they are ripe otherwise they will fall, rot or be eaten by birds.

Strawberries

Few crops are more satisfying to grow than strawberries! Not only do they look wonderful, but they taste far better than anything you will ever buy.

Suitable Containers

Strawberries are perfect for any gardener, regardless of size of plot because they will thrive in virtually any container. You can grow them in hanging baskets, growbags or even buy specially designed strawberry planters. If you want to grow them in window boxes, make sure the container is a minimum of 20 cm (8 in) so it can hold enough water.

Soil

Strawberries like a fertile, well-drained soil.

Top Tip

Do not wash strawberries until you are ready to eat them; moisture is the main enemy of strawberries.

Care and Position

Plant strawberry plants late spring or early summer when all risk of frost has passed. Strawberries like full sun and should have straw placed around the plants to keep moisture in the soil and to allow the fruits to grow up off the soil. They will tolerate cold winters, but you can cover them with fleece if the weather is particularly harsh. Strawberries do not like cold, wet climates, so protect them in such cases.

Varieties

Early strawberries varieties include 'Christine' which has good mildew resistance. 'Cambridge Favourite' is popular with beginners because it is disease resistant and reliable; it is ready to

harvest mid season. 'Judibell' is ready very late in the season. If you successfully grow one of each of these varieties, you can be enjoying strawberries from late spring to early autumn.

Pests and Diseases

Strawberries are prone to mould, but keeping the fruits off the soil with a layer of straw can help. Slugs and birds enjoy strawberries so you will need to protect them from being eaten with netting and perhaps slug pellets.

Harvest

Strawberries are ripe when the fruits are completely red. Don't leave them too long otherwise they can start to rot or get eaten by birds. Once picked, enjoy them fresh with sugar and cream or mix into smoothies. If you grow enough, strawberry jam is delicious.

Gooseberries

Good news! If your growing area has little sun and warmth you can still grow fruit! Gooseberries will tolerate cold weather admirably and are pretty unfussy about soil conditions too.

Suitable Containers

Prepare a 30 cm (12 in) pot with a layer of crocks and then some free-draining material such as gravel before topping up with compost.

Soil

Gooseberries need good drainage, but the quality of the compost is not important. As long as it is disease free, you can use old compost for your gooseberry bushes.

Care and Position

Plant gooseberry bushes during early autumn and prune them in late winter. Each autumn,

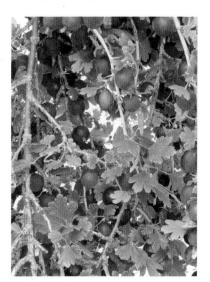

scrape off the top few inches of compost and replace with fresh. Gooseberries do not like to be over watered, so you must make sure the container drains well. Feed every month during the growing season.

Pruning

Prune mid winter and take out any crowded branches. If the fruit grows too close together it can rot.

Varieties

'Hinnonmaki Red' is great for beginners because it is virtually resistant to mildew.

'Hinnonmaki Red' is a good gooseberry option for beginners.

Pests and Diseases

Gooseberries can suffer from botrytis; the way to avoid this is with good pruning and picking off small fruits if they are growing too close to others. Good air circulation is the key. Also, once the berries start to ripen, keep an eye on them and make sure they are healthy. If they start to get mildew, pick them all and preserve the good ones by cooking into jam or freezing for later use.

Harvest

When you harvest gooseberries depends on what you want to do with them. If you're going to eat them fresh, you don't want them too sour, but if you're going to make jams or syrups you can pick them as soon as they begin to soften.

Autumn-fruiting Raspberries

Autumn-fruiting raspberries are ideal for containers because they like free-draining soil. If their roots get too wet they rot easily. There are two types of raspberries; those that fruit in summer and those that fruit in autumn. Autumn-fruiting raspberries are easier to manage in containers because they don't need any support.

Suitable Containers

Select a large pot around 45 cm (18 in).

Did You Know?

Not all raspberries are red! You can buy gold, yellow, purple and black versions too.

Soil

Raspberries like rich compost and need firmly planting; really firm them in and plant deep into the soil. As they like good quality soil, replace as much of the soil as possible every year. If you can get hold of it, well-rotted manure is a great addition to the compost when planting your raspberries.

Care and Position

Plant raspberry bushes in mid autumn and keep in a sheltered spot. While raspberries prefer full sun, it's worth trying them if you have a less-than-sunny spot as they can tolerate shade. Water them regularly to ensure the fruits swell.

Pruning

Cut plants down to 10 cm (4 in) during the winter and your plant will flourish.

Varieties

'Autumn Bliss' produces short canes that don't need supporting in sheltered areas. The berries are large, heavy cropping and have a good flavour.

'Autumn Bliss' rasberries need little support.

Pests and Diseases

Aphids can be a problem on raspberries; keep an eye out for them and rub off gently with your finger and thumb or carefully use a jet of water to blast them off, but don't damage the delicate fruits.

Harvest

Raspberries are ready when they pull away easily from the bush. Once they start to ripen you'll need to get there before the birds do. Raspberries are delicious eaten fresh or added to smoothies and they freeze well too.

Herbs

Herbs are an excellent crop for novices and are the perfect solution for tiny gardens. You can grow them in individual pots inside your home – why not try a few basic herbs on your kitchen windowsill? They are suitable for outside window boxes, hanging baskets, planters of all sizes and larger plants such as fennel can be planted in raised beds. This section deals with a few commonly used culinary herbs.

Basil

Basil, with its distinctive taste, is a lovely summer herb. The best place to grow basil is indoors on a sunny windowsill, but it will grow well in window boxes and patio containers in a sheltered spot, as long as you have a long, hot summer.

Growing from Seed

Basil is sown directly into pots of rich, moist free-draining soil on a sunny windowsill. Once seedlings have established they can be hardened off and transplanted after all risks of frost have passed – early summer is best. You can warm the soil in pots by using cloches.

Top Tip

Cover basil leaves with water and freeze – add at the end of cooking meals to impart flavour.

Position and Soil

The secret with Mediterranean herbs is well-draining soil in full sun. Pots of basil are well suited to sun trap areas of your plot or against a south-facing wall.

Care of Basil

A top tip for getting the watering just right with basil is to wait for the plant to slightly wilt before giving it a good drink. In other words, let the plant tell *you* when it needs watering. Some days it will need daily watering, but at cooler times it may not need much water at all. The worst thing you can do is over water basil or leave its roots standing in water. Pinch out the tips and take off the flowers before they produce seeds for a continual supply. Once the seeds set the basil will stop growing. Take as many leaves as you like; they'll soon grow again if conditions are favourable.

Basil flowers should be pinched out before they set to seed.

Pests and Diseases

Slugs may be a problem, but basil isn't their favourite plant. If your basil is troubled by slugs, protect the plants with barriers or traps.

Varieties

'Greek' basil produces small plants with lots of tiny leaves. 'Genovese' is the best variety for making pesto.

Did You Know?

The ancient Greeks and Romans believed if you left a basil leaf under a pot, it would turn into a scorpion.

Coriander

Commonly used in Indian cooking, coriander is a popular herb. It is easy to grow and will happily survive indoors or outdoors.

Growing from Seed

Sow coriander every three to four weeks, in situ, for a continual supply. Sow in pots of moist multi-purpose compost. Sprinkle seed evenly over the compost and cover with 1 cm (½ in) of compost before watering well. Thin out seedlings to around 5 cm (2 in) between plants.

Position and Soil

Coriander likes sun but will appreciate some shade in very hot weather; it is ideal for growing in the dappled shade of other plants. Keep well watered in very hot weather.

Care of Coriander

The leaves are ready to be picked when the plants are around 10–15 cm (4–6 in) tall. You can leave the plant to produce new leaves. Harvest the leaves regularly from April to September for the best tasting crop.

Pests and Diseases

Coriander does not tend to suffer from pests and diseases.

Varieties

'Coriander Lemon' is a fast-growing sweet coriander with a subtle lemon flavour which is not as bitter as other coriander varieties. It is highly recommended for pots.

Did You Know?

Coriander is mentioned as an aphrodisiac in The Tales of the Arabian Nights.

Mint

Mint is perfect for containers because many gardeners view mint as a weed – give it space and it will happily take over. Growing mint in a pot contains the growth and keeps leaves small and tender. It is also the ideal crop for novices and children because it is easy to take care of and quick to grow.

Growing from Seed

Although mint can be grown from seed (sow seeds in situ in pots of any type of soil), the easiest way to grow it is from a cutting from a friend. Simply take a sprig or two, pop it in a container of soil, keep it watered and it will take root easily.

Position and Soil

Mint is not fussy about soil type and can tolerate most conditions, although it prefers moisture-retentive soils. It will grow in semi-shade too, which makes it ideal for some plots that don't get much sun.

Care of Mint

Mint likes to be kept moist so keep an eye on watering, although it can withstand most conditions and treatment once established. The more you harvest mint, the more it grows so you can be heavy handed with taking leaves. Remove the heads before they flower to keep the plant growing. It will even grow throughout the winter when there is not much left in the garden.

Pests and Diseases

Mint is not troubled by many pests and diseases as it is so robust.

Varieties

'Spearmint' is the well-known mint served with peas and potatoes and to make mint sauce. It is also the best type of mint for herbal tea.

Top Tip

Hang bunches of mint in your home to prevent flies in the summer.

Parsley

Parsley isn't ideal for beginners because it can be difficult to germinate. However, it is a great plant for window boxes and containers.

Growing from Seed

Parsley is notoriously difficult to germinate, but this doesn't mean you shouldn't try! One trick is to soak the seeds in room temperature water a couple of hours before sowing. Sow the seeds in situ in containers of rich compost once the soil and air temperature has warmed up. Traditionally, parsley seed is sown on Good Friday (the only day the Devil does not rule the soil!). If you don't succeed with germination then buy a plant from a garden centre.

Curly parsley.

Position and Soil

Parsley needs rich, moist soil and likes a damp or semi-shaded position. This makes it ideal for plots that don't get full sun and means parsley can be planted in the dappled shade of other crops.

Care of Parsley

Parsley must be kept moist otherwise it will die quickly; the leaves turn brown and wither. Water it regularly but lightly and pick off the leaves as you need them – new leaves will grow back.

Pests and Diseases

Parsley does not tend to suffer from pests and diseases.

Varieties

'Champion' is a popular curly-leaved parsley that can be grown indoors on a sunny windowsill. 'French' has flat leaves and is reputed to have better flavour than curled.

Flat-leaved parsley.

Chives

Chives are a very useful crop to grow, not just to eat but because they can ward off pests from other plants. Chives are one of the most commonly used herbs and have a mild onion flavour.

Did You Know?

Parsley is a natural breath freshener – chew on a sprig after a meal, especially one containing lots of garlic!

Growing from Seed

Chives can be grown in pots indoors on a sunny windowsill from March (early spring) or outdoors in pots and window boxes during May (late spring). Sow the seed 0.5 cm deep and keep seedlings densely growing for a cut-and-come-again crop. Chives are a simple crop for both novice gardeners and children to take care of.

Position and Soil

Chives like rich, well-drained soil in full sun and grow well in pots.

Care of Chives

Chives must be well watered in dry weather. Cut back the plants regularly to prevent the purple flowers growing; once these grow the chives become woody and not so tender to eat. Having said that, if you're growing chives outdoors, bees and butterflies love the flowers, so why not grow a few pots, let some flower and keep others harvested for yourself? Harvest when the leaves are small and tender; if you leave 5 cm (2 in) of the leaf in the soil it will grow again. Leaves are ready for eating around 12 weeks after sowing.

Encourage bees and butterflies by allowing some of your chive plants to flower.

Pests and Diseases

Chives do not tend to suffer from pests and diseases; in fact they can help deter pests from other crops.

Varieties

'Garlic Chives' have a mild garlic flavour and can be used to ward off aphids, mites and carrot fly from other crops.

Did you know?

The attractive purple chive flowers can be eaten too. Why not serve as a salad garnish?

Edible Flowers

Most people associate container gardening with pretty flowers and there is no reason why your edible container garden shouldn't contain them. Not only do some attract bees and other beneficial insects, but many can also be eaten. Use them to garnish salads and add colour to your plate.

Careful Choices

You must know what you are eating when trying flowers as some are poisonous. Buy your plants or seed from a reputable source and make sure you know what you have sown. Some people who have allergic reactions (hayfever or asthma) to certain flowers shouldn't eat them or any members of the same flower family.

How to Use Edible Flowers

There are numerous flowers that are suitable for eating; this is just a small selection. There are also several ways to use them in the kitchen – here are some ideas:

- Scatter the petals and leaves into salads.
- Freeze whole flowers into ice cubes for adding to drinks.
- Infuse the flowers in oils or vinegars.
- Make flowers into tea.
- Add chopped flowers to omelettes or pizza.

Chamomile Petals

With its faint apple aroma and taste, you can use chamomile petals as a tea. Simply infuse a teaspoon of chamomile petals in a cup of boiling water for 10 minutes, strain and drink. Chamomile is relaxing, so it makes a great drink to have before bed or is useful in times of stress.

Chive Flowers

The beautiful purple chive flowers are very attractive to bees and butterflies so make sure you share your crop! You can eat them with salads to provide a mild onion flavour or add to omelettes or soups. If you pull apart the petals you can mix them into butter for a mild version of garlic butter.

Courgette Flowers

Courgette flowers can be used like vine leaves or cabbage leaves and eaten with a filling. Stuff them with your chosen mix (ricotta and mint is a popular choice), dip in batter, then fry until golden. Alternatively treat the courgette flowers like spinach; shred finely, toss in hot oil until wilted and serve with rice.

Nasturtium

The flowers, seeds and leaves can all be eaten on nasturtium plants. Nasturtium flowers make a wonderful addition to salads with their bright, cheery colours. They have a peppery taste, a bit like watercress. The seeds can be pickled and used like capers and the leaves can be used as salad leaves.

Pot Marigolds (Calendula officinalis)

Known as 'poor man's saffron' Calendula petals are used to add a beautiful colour to dishes such as cooked rice and pasta. Some people also use the petals in milk recipes to add a deep, golden colour.

Did you know?

There are enough different types of lettuce to grow them all year round.

Roses

Both rose petals and rose hips can be used in the kitchen. You must remove the white part of the petals because they are bitter, but the main part can be eaten or made into rose petal jam. Rosehips are very high in vitamin C and are used to make syrups or tea.

Other Flowers

There are many other flowers that are edible including the following:

- ☑ **Violet leaves and flowers.**
- ☑ **Chrysanthemum flowers.**
- ☑ **Citrus blossom flowers.**
- ☑ **Pansy petals.**
- ☑ **Cornflowers.**
- ☑ **Lavender flowers.**

Violets make an attractive salad garnish.

Checklist

Remember to consider the following for successful fruit crops:

☑ **Space**: How much space do you have to grow fruit? Could you grow a large fruit tree or do you only have room for a hanging basket of strawberries?

☑ **Containers**: Do you have large enough containers for fruit trees? If you are growing on a balcony or rooftop is the surface strong enough to support large containers full of soil.

☑ **Harvesting**: Are you generally around during harvest time? Once many fruits ripen, birds will be attracted to them so you need to be there to pick them.

☑ **Indoor plants**: Are you growing food indoors? If so, a citrus tree is ideal.

☑ **Shade**: If your plot is shady, try gooseberries along with some shade-tolerant herbs such as mint.

☑ **Growing herbs**: Take a look at your kitchen shelves – which herbs do you regularly buy? Perhaps you could grow your own this year!

☑ **Edible flowers**: If you want a pretty garden, growing edible flowers is the perfect way to achieve this; not only do they look nice, but they attract beneficial insects too.

Frugal
Gardening

Economical Ideas

Although gardening can be very expensive, especially when setting up for the first time, there are many ways to make your container garden an economical activity. As more and more people try to budget their finances carefully, there's never been a better time to grow some of your own food! In this chapter you'll discover ways, from seed to harvest, to make gardening an economical activity that might even pay for itself.

Compost

If you have to buy compost from a garden centre to fill your containers, it can be expensive. There are several ways to reduce this cost and the best one is to make your own. By making your own compost you help close the loop by turning 'rubbish' into a valuable resource on site. It's easy to make compost; in a suitable container, layer 'green' items such as grass clippings and vegetable peelings with 'brown' items such as shredded cardboard and twigs. Mix it up, give it a stir every few weeks and in a few months you'll get good compost to use in your containers.

Compost for Free

If you don't have space for your own compost heap, it's worth asking friends, colleagues or your local Freecycle group (www.freecycle.org). Many people make compost but don't need all of it for themselves. You may be able to take what you need in exchange for donating your food scraps and decayed plant growth or by offering to help make the compost throughout the year. If you have room for a bokashi bin at home you could offer to donate your fermented foods – these make an excellent addition to the compost heap.

Small-scale Composting

If your space is very limited you could set up a wormery. These consist of several stacking layers where worms live, eat and produce vermicompost. After a few months of regular feeding and maintenance, the bottom layer contains vermicompost, the middle layer contains material currently being digested by the worms and the top layer is where you add new waste. Complete kits can be bought from garden centres and online stores or you can make your own.

Keeping it Local

Some local authorities sell compost to their residents. Although it's not always consistent in quality and is used more as a soil conditioner than compost, it's useful for 'diluting' more expensive compost for crops that don't need too many nutrients. You can often purchase it at your local household recycling centre.

Bulk Buying

Like many things in life, buying compost in bulk can provide you with significant savings. Some companies will deliver bulk bags containing a cubic metre of compost. This can be a great way to buy because it's often made fresh to your specification, using the John Innes formulae. The bags are delivered to the kerbside on a pallet, so you'll need to have good access to your property. If you can't manage a large bag, ask at your local garden centre; they will sometimes deliver a pallet of individual compost bags which are easier to manage and cheaper to buy.

Compost Savings

Buying ready-prepared compost can be costly – here are some ways to reduce the cost:

- **Make your own compost; it's free!**
- **Buy from your local authority.**
- **Buy in bulk and have it delivered to your home.**
- **See if a friend or neighbour would be willing to share theirs.**
- **Set up a small wormery if you don't have room for a compost bin.**

Containers and Tools

Saving money on suitable growing containers is a lot of fun, creative and easy to do. All you need to do is scour your home for anything that can have holes drilled in the bottom and can hold a reasonable amount of soil! Finding suitable seedling containers is particularly easy because they don't have to be very big – old yogurt pots or margarine tubs are perfect. Tools can be one of the most expensive investments when setting up an edible garden, but fortunately growing food in containers reduces this cost.

Ideas for Containers

Bathroom Suites

Old baths, Belfast sinks and even old toilet bowls are great containers for growing crops. They last a long time because the materials do not corrode and they can make an amazing display. They are a fun and creative way to grow food and add an element of art to your patio or garden. The disadvantage is the weight as they can be quite heavy.

Footwear

Do your boots leak or your Wellingtons let in the rain? These can make quirky containers for food; just imagine strawberries spilling out of a pair of Wellies! Admittedly you won't get much food from one shoe, but they make a good conversation piece and are a lovely idea for children.

Kitchen Supplies

Has your favourite saucepan lost its handle or have you broken the lid? Do you have an empty wooden apple or wine crate? How about the nets your citrus fruit was bought in? Do you have a heavyweight shopping bag that has lost its handle or a wicker basket that has seen better days? All of these items make wonderful containers. Wooden crates and wicker baskets are particularly attractive. These types of containers are not very deep so are better suited to plants with short roots such as herbs. Fruit nets can be hung on the wall and used as hanging baskets; they are ideal for tumbling tomatoes.

Did you Know?

Terracotta means 'baked earth' because it is made from clay. The first clay sculptures were sun dried; long before the days of kilns!

Garden Equipment

What about that rusty wheelbarrow that has a few holes in the bottom or the bucket that leaks? These make fantastic containers. Wheelbarrows are a good height from the ground, making them attractive for people who find it hard to bend or kneel. Using old buckets is a great form of reuse, helping reduce the amount of waste you send to landfill. Buckets are ideal for planting a few carrots, while wheelbarrows lend themselves to salad leaves.

Use Your Imagination

Do you have a stack of tyres or some large builders' merchant bags? Or maybe an old dustbin (trash can) that you no longer use? These are large items which are ideal for growing bigger crops. A stack of tyres lends itself beautifully to growing potatoes – you can add another tyre as the crop needs it. You can grow anything in a large builders' merchant bag; even some of the smaller squashes or courgettes. Old dustbins are ideal for a few carrots. How about making your own containers from pallets or half barrels?

Furniture

People make planters from all sorts of items – old wardrobes, drawers, even floorboards that have been replaced. The wood might not last forever but at least you are giving an old piece of furniture a new lease of life. The beauty of using these types of containers is you can make them any size you want. You can even make 'made to measure' for your specific plot.

Advantages of Reused Pots

There are several benefits of reusing pots:

- Pots can be sourced for free.
- Reusing helps reduce landfill waste.
- You can create unique containers.

Disadvantages of Reused pots

There are some drawbacks to recycling:

- Old pots can look ugly or mismatched.
- Many items from the home are small or shallow.
- Reusing requires thought; it's more convenient to buy from a store.

Tools

You don't need large, expensive pieces of equipment when growing in containers and if you really need to, an old tablespoon from your kitchen drawer will do as a temporary trowel!

Second-hand Savings

Many people have old tools, containers or even seeds they no longer need. Start asking friends, family, colleagues and neighbours to see what you can get for free. If someone is sorting out their shed, they'll only be happy to see their unwanted items going to a new, enthusiastic owner. And most people will happily share and lend in exchange for some of your home-grown goodies. Try scouring local antiques shops, charity shops and jumble sales for useful gardening items. Perhaps you'll pick up some gloves, unusual pots, a gardening calendar or some preserving items to get you started.

Car Boot Sales

Car boot sales, garage sales and yard sales are some of the best places to source second-hand tools. You'll be able to get everything you need for much less money than buying new. You might get lucky and find yourself with some really old, yet well-made tools; the sort that might be difficult to get hold of today.

Seeds and Plants

Getting seeds and plants for free is pretty straightforward. Almost all gardeners get carried away when buying seeds and end up with excess! In addition, most people sow far too many seeds and find themselves with more plants than they can manage.

Freebies

Do you have friends who subscribe to magazines or do you buy them yourself? Often seeds are given away on the front of magazines or are offered in newspapers where you fill in a form and they send them to you. You may have to pay postage but you usually get a reasonable amount of seeds for this.

Online Offers

There are numerous organizations that set up campaigns throughout the year in order to encourage people to grow their own food. The BBC have their 'Dig In' campaign once a year where participants can get five different types of seed; usually carrots, along with other 'easy to grow' items such as lettuce, beans or basil. Garden Organic runs their 'One Pot Pledge' where they encourage people who have never grown anything to try.

Seed Swap Sites

Another way to get free seeds online is to participate in a seed swap. There are numerous gardening forums or ones dedicated solely to seed swapping. Members advertise any excess seeds they have and other members can contact them to arrange collection or postage. The great thing about seed swaps is that they are cheap and easy to send in the post.

Freecycle

Freecycle is a wonderful worldwide organization (www.freecycle.org) where you can give and get things for free. For anyone setting up a garden it can be an invaluable resource. Not only can you get containers and gardening tools, but you can be sure to find someone offering seeds and vegetable plants. LETS is another organization where people 'barter' instead of using money. You could swap some home-made cookies for a few seed packets. Both schemes are a great way of meeting local people with similar interests.

Local Groups

As more and more people become aware of environmental challenges there is a growing trend towards a more self-sufficient lifestyle. Growing food is an obvious starting place and there are lots of local community groups who are sharing knowledge, skills and tools. You may find a transition town or local gardening club nearby where you can glean invaluable information about growing food and other aspects of self-sufficiency. You'll find seed swapping is part of the 'norm' in gardening clubs.

Sharing the Load

If you have a few friends or colleagues who garden you can club together to buy seed. You could each buy three different crop types and share them out. This is a valuable way to save resources and money and a little 'competitive' spirit is great to keep you accountable for taking care of your crop! If one of you has limited space and the other has an allotment you could share what you grow. Someone could grow potatoes for everyone, whereas the person with limited space could grow and dry herbs.

As Nature Intended

Once you've had one successful gardening year you'll be able to start saving your seeds. Some are more straightforward than others. Easy seeds to save are runner beans and courgettes. Others are trickier and you can work your way up to saving seeds that need special treatment as your confidence grows. Store fresh, dry seed in paper bags or envelopes in the refrigerator until the following year.

Nature's Bounty

There are numerous ways to get free seeds – here are some ideas:

- Some magazines offer them as free gifts.
- Campaigns such as BBC 'Dig In' or Garden Organic's 'One Pot Pledge' give participants seeds for free.
- Online seed swap sites and gardening forums.
- Freecycle or local timebanks are a great way to get free seeds.
- Community networks such as transition towns or local gardening clubs often organize seed swaps.
- Arrange with a friend that you will go halves on seeds.
- Seed saving is the most self-sufficient option – have a go at simple seeds such as runner beans.

Plants

Not only is it easy to get free seeds, but most gardeners end up with far more plants than they can manage too. It's always wise to sow more seed than you need to allow for failures with germination, but sometimes you hit lucky and every plant thrives, which means you then need to give them away.

Plant Swaps

Just like you can swap seeds, most gardeners are only too happy to swap plants. If you've had a particularly successful germination of one crop you can bet your friends or neighbours have had success with a different one. Plant sales take place regularly, so you could even *sell* your excess.

Plant Care

Regular watering, feeding and treating plants can soon add up. By the time you've paid your water bill, bought fertilizers and invested in certain pesticides or disease treatments you can be forgiven for thinking gardening is a hobby for people with a large disposable income. However, there are several ways to reduce the amount of money you spend on plant care and what's more, they benefit the environment too, making gardening a truly green hobby.

Watering

We have to pay to get water into our homes through the taps, but it falls freely out of the sky in most countries. One way to reduce your dependency on tap water is to store rain water. You can buy rain barrels in all sorts of sizes to fit even the smallest plot. All you need is a down pipe to direct into the water barrel and a tap to get it back out with. Some plants prefer rain water so you won't be able to grow them unless you can capture rain water effectively.

Irrigation

If you want a self-watering garden or fancy irrigation system, there are plenty of ways to do this without costing much at all. You can either make yourself self-watering containers or set up a system with old plastic bottles. Using old plastic bottles is the perfect way to get water to the roots of plants such as tomatoes, peppers and aubergines.

Using Plastic Bottles

If you want to make watering less of a chore, try the plastic bottle method of watering and see if it helps you:

- **Wash an old 2 litre plastic bottle.**
- **Put the cap on and drill two small holes in the cap.**
- **Cut the bottom third off the bottle.**
- **Insert the bottle at a 45 degree angle next to the plant you want to water, being careful not to damage the roots of any established plants.**
- **Fill your bottle with water and it will deliver a trickle of water to the roots of your plant!**

Wicking

Using wicking is another good way to water plants and ensure they get enough water. It's simple and free to set up. All you need is an old jar and a piece of cotton string or length of cotton material – an old cotton T-shirt cut into strips is ideal. Put your jar next to the plant you want to keep watered and fill with water. Put one end of the string or cotton material into the jar and drape the other end onto the soil of the plant you want to water. The moisture will wick up the string and into the soil of your plant.

Fertilizers

You'll be aware that container-grown crops need much more care and feeding from you than those in open soil. Regular feeding, especially during a busy growing season can soon leave you out of pocket. Fortunately, nature provides plant food and it's pretty too! Comfrey is every gardener's best friend. It's virtually impossible to kill, attracts bees to your garden which help pollinate crops and it can be made into an excellent fertilizer.

Comfrey Fertilizer

Making comfrey fertilizer isn't the most sociable of activities as it really stinks! But it is worth doing to save money and help the environment. All you need to do is steep comfrey leaves in a bucket of rain water, cover and leave for a few weeks before straining and adding new leaves to the water. Strain it again and bottle. Dilute this fertilizer 20 times with water.

Pesticides

Pesticides are used by gardeners and farmers to kill, prevent or deter pests. Most are made from synthetic chemicals and are not only toxic to the pests, but can be toxic to the environment and your health. In addition, pesticides can be expensive and add a considerable amount to your gardening budget.

Natural Methods

Before the widespread use of synthetic pesticides, farmers used natural methods such as companion planting and encouraging natural predators to their land. In other words, they paid special attention to the complete ecosystem.

Companion Planting

Companion planting means you plant certain plants in close proximity to one another. These companion plants might be planted for several reasons such as:

- **Repelling pests**: If you remember from previous chapters, one of the worst pests for carrots is the carrot fly. These are attracted to the smell of carrot leaves. By 'masking' the scent of the leaves you can repel the pest from causing trouble. Chives and garlic are excellent crops for protecting against the carrot fly.

- **Sacrificial plants**: If you find slugs heading for your spinach plants you can sow sacrificial crops around them. By sowing cheap lettuce seed, the slugs will eat your lettuces and hopefully leave most of your spinach alone for you to enjoy!

- **Attracting insects**: Some insects such as bees help pollinate food. Other insects like ladybirds feed on garden pests. By attracting beneficial insects to your garden you can increase yields and reduce the risk of pest damage. Plant a container with comfrey to attract bees and use as a garden fertilizer. Plant dill or yarrow for ladybirds.

- **Enhancing flavour**: Some plants are reported to enhance the flavour of others. For example growing basil next to tomatoes makes them taste better, yarrow increases the essential oils in some herbs which gives them more flavour and chervil can add a peppery taste to radishes.

Top Tip

Save plastic bag ties, or cut old clothes into strips for securing plants to canes instead of buying plant ties from a garden centre.

Checklist

Recap on money-saving ideas:

✓ **Compost**: Is there room on your gardening plot for a small compost heap or wormery? This is a great way to save money on buying compost.

✓ **Bulk-buying**: Purchasing compost in bulk from an online supplier or local garden centre can save you a lot of money.

✓ **Recycling pots**: Start saving old yogurt pots, margarine containers or plastic water bottles for sowing seeds.

✓ **Reusing**: Take a look in your garage or shed and see what you could use as a suitable container for your garden.

✓ **Saving seeds**: Some plants are easy to gather your own seeds from, such as runner beans. Why not keep half a dozen and try sowing them next year?

✓ **Seed swaps**: Find out about a local LETS group and see if they hold seed swaps throughout the year.

✓ **Second-hand bargains**: Start asking friends, family and colleagues to see if they are clearing out the shed or garage; you might find they have some tools to give you!

✓ **Charity shops**: Visit charity shops, car boot sales and yard sales for old tools and other gardening and preserving equipment.

Further Reading

Barker, B., *Container Gardening for Health: The 12 Most Important Fruits and Vegetables for your Organic Garden*, Prairie Oak Publishing, 2009

Brennan, G., Luebbermann, M., and Echtermeyer, F., *Little Herb Gardens: Simple Secrets for Glorious Gardens – Indoors and Out*, Chronicle Books, 1993

Caplin, J., *Urban Eden: Grow Delicious Fruit, Vegetables and Herbs in a Really Small Space*, Kyle Cathie, 2004

Container Gardening: 250 Design Ideas & Step-By-Step Techniques, Taunton Press, 2009

Crandall, C., *Movable Harvests: The Simplicity & Bounty of Container Gardens*, Houghton Mifflin, 1995

Guerra, M., *The Edible Container Garden: Fresh Food from Tiny Spaces*, Gaia Books Ltd, 2005

Harrison, J., *Vegetable, Fruit and Herb Growing in Small Spaces*, Right Way, 2010

Herda, D.J., *From Container to Kitchen: Growing Fruits and Vegetables in Pots*, New Society Publishers, 2010

Loewer, P., *Small Space Gardening: How to Successfully Grow Flowers and Fruits in Containers and Pots*, Lyons Press, 2004

McGee, R.M.N., and Stuckey, M., *McGee and Stuckey's Bountiful Container: Create Container Gardens of Vegetables, Herbs. Fruits, and Edible Flowers*, Workman Publishing Company, 2002

Moore, J., *Gardeners' World: 101 Ideas for Veg from Small Spaces*, BBC Books, 2009

Peacock, P., *Patio Produce: How to Cultivate a Lot of Home-grown Vegetables from the Smallest Possible Space*, Spring Hill, 2009

Purnell, B., *Crops in Pots: 50 Great Container Projects Using Vegetables, Fruit, and Herbs*, Hamlyn, 2007

Purnell, B., *Crops in Pots: How to Plan, Plant, and Grow Vegetables, Fruits, and Herbs in Easy-Care Containers*, Reader's Digest Children's Publishing, 2007

Schneebeli-Morr, D., *Grow Your Own Herbs in Pots: 35 Simple Projects for Creating Beautiful Container Herb Gardens*, Cico, 2010

Schneebeli-Morrell, D., *Organic Crops in Pots: How to Grow Your Own Fruit, Vegetables, and Herbs*, CICO Books, 2009

Trail, G., *Grow Great Grub: Organic Food from Small Spaces*, Clarkson Potter, 2010

Websites

www.backyardgardener.com
A cornucopia of growing tips, the site also includes a comprehensive gardening dictionary and green-themed poetry section.

www.bbc.co.uk/digin
The BBC's online campaign encourages domestic vegetable cultivation and cooking in a fun, accessible manner.

www.bbc.co.uk/gardenersworld
Fans of the long-serving television show can revisit clips and discover a range of supplementary gardening information.

www.bbc.co.uk/gardening/basics/techniques/
The BBC's gardening homepage provides basic growing techniques for the budding gardener.

www.container-gardens.com
A small site dedicated to everything for container gardening.

www.davesgarden.com
Established "for gardeners, by gardeners," the site provides handy tips and helpful hints from its members, along with a list of approved online product websites.

www.finegardening.com
A great source of information for container gardening how-to and design, as well as articles and tips on all different gardening styles.

www.gardeners.com
Garden supplies, gardening tools, and gardening tips for home gardeners.

www.gardenguides.com
A detailed plant directory is accompanied by an invaluable pest-management section.

www.gardenorganic.org.uk
Garden Organic is a national charity promoting organic gardening and food.

www.gardensupplies.co.uk
Offers an extensive range of garden supplies.

www.growingtaste.com
A useful resource for growers particularly keen to maximize the flavour of their vegetable crop.

www.kitchengardeners.org
Hosting a series of links to individual growing and cookery blogs, the site supports a global gardening community.

www.nickys-nursery.co.uk
Nicky's Nursery provides a catalogue of great value seed packets, complemented by a helpful vegetable sowing calendar.

www.rhs.org.uk
Royal Horticultural Society website offering an extensive range of gardening advice, from cultivation to pest control, as well as a forum allowing you to post personal tips and have your queries answered.

www.unwins.co.uk
Unwins is a valuable online supplier of vegetable seeds, all carefully selected and picked by hand.

www.veggiegardeningtips.com
Offers organic growing techniques and recommended gardening products in a personal and approachable style.

Index

A

air drying 140
aluminium containers 91
aphids 152–54, 177, 179, 180, 216, 223
apples 211–12
aubergines 179–80
autumn 98

B

baby sweetcorn 184–85
balconies 33
basil 39, 224–25
beans 140, 181–84
beetroot (beet) 39, 129, 134, 186–87
biodegradable pots 85–87, 109
blackfly 152–54, 182
blanching 144–45
blight 160–61, 191
blossom end rot 161, 179
blueberry plants 212–14
bokashi bin 238
bolting 129
botrytis 162–63, 180, 222
bottling 147
broad beans 181–82
Brussels sprouts 33
budgeting 30, 71–72

C

cabbage whites 154–55, 205
calendula petals 233
canker 190, 212
carrot fly 155–57, 188, 190
carrots 134, 187–89
caterpillars 155, 205
chamomile petals 232
chard 133, 202–203
chillies 35
chive flowers 232
chives 229–30
chutney 147
citrus fruit 214–16
clearing up 166
cloches 122
coir 104
coir pots 86
comfrey fertilizer 249
companion planting 250
compost 21, 40–49, 77, 96, 104, 164, 238–39
conservatories 35, 214
containers 65, 78–95, 94–96, 124, 211, 215, 219, 221, 240–43
convenience 19, 51
coriander 226–27
courgette flowers 233
courgettes 20, 143, 165, 193–94
cranberry plants 212–14
crop selection 56–60
cucumbers 39, 165, 194–95

D

damping off 163–64
dehydrators 140
dietary needs 58–60, 63
diseases 21, 27, 160–66, *see also* individual plant types
doorsteps 36
drainage 95, 115
drought 65
drying food 137–41
dwarf beans 183–84

E

earthing up 191, 201
edible flowers 231–34
eggplants *see* aubergines
energy 68–70
environmental issues 24–26, 169–72
ericaceous compost 46
exercise 12

F

family food 57
fava beans *see* broad beans
feeding 116–19
fennel 154
fertilizer/nutrients 31, 43, 44, 77, 117–19, 248–49
fibreglass containers 82–83
figs 216–17
flea beetle 192
foliage wilting 128
food

bills 23
drying 137–41
miles 24–25
packaging 26
storage 132–36
transportation 25
waste 26
Freecycle 245
freezer containers 144
freezing 129, 135,
142–46, 194
freshness 130–31, 135
frost damage 131
fruit storage 136
fruit trees 210–23
fungicides 163, 165, 195, 196

G
garden centres 66
gardening year 97–98
garlic 128, 133, 197–8
gooseberries 221–22
greenfly 152–54
ground control 20–22
growbags 45
growing season 21, 121–24
growth space 50

H
hanging baskets 34, 62
hardening off 110–111
harvesting 128–31
herbs 35, 39, 135, 224–30
horticultural fleece 36, 122,
156, 188, 192, 199, 205
horticultural grit 48
hygiene 164

I
inorganic fertilizers 117

insulation 121
intensive farming 172
invasive growers 20
irrigation 247

J
John Innes compost 42, 43,
44, 49

K
kale 39, 133, 202, 204–205

L
labelling 146
ladybirds 153
leeks 198–99
lemons 214–16
lettuce 132, 233
lettuce spinach 39
light 38–39
limes 214–16

M
maggots 199
masking 156
meal planning 56
mice 185
mildew 165–66, 194, 195,
201, 203, 212, 222
mint 20, 227–28
misters 107
money matters 30, 71–72
mould 220
multi-cells 103
multi-purpose compost 44

N
nasturtium 233
net curtains 36

nutrients/fertilizer 31, 43, 44,
77, 117–19, 248–49

O
onion fly 199, 201
onions 39, 59, 128, 133,
200–201
oranges 214–16
organic fertilizers 117
organic growing 169–72
over-wintering 131

P
parsley 157, 228–29
parsnips 144, 157, 189–90
patios 33
pears 217–18
peas 64
peat conservation 46
peat-based compost 45–46
peppers 34, 35, 39, 178–79
perlite 48
permaculture 69, 89
pesticides 169–72, 249–50
pests 21, 27, 152–59, 250,
see also individual
plant types
planning 30–32, 68
plant care 247–50
plant swaps 246
plastic containers 78–80
pollination 185
polythene 123
polytunnels 123
pot jackets 123
pot marigolds 233
potato blight 160, 191
potatoes 128, 134,
171, 190–91
pots 21, 78–95, 103, 242

potting compost 43
potting on 110
powdery mildew 165–66,
    194, 195, 203
preserving 147–48
pruning 212, 213, 218,
    221, 223
pull test 108–109
PVC pots 81

R
radishes 39, 129, 191–92
raised beds 88–9
raspberries 222–23
recycling 72, 80, 85, 87
red spider mite 157–58, 179,
    180, 216
refrigeration 135
rice husk pots 21
roof gardens 33, 64
root vegetables 186–92
roses 234
runner beans 183–84
rust 199, 212

S
sacrificial plants 154,
    206, 250
salad leaves 132, 205–206
sand 48
scab 212
scallions *see* spring onions
seasonal food 22
seed 31, 32, 43, 52, 76, 180,
    244–45
    compost 43
    sowing 102–107
    storage 52, 104
    swaps 244
    tapes 124

trays 102–103
seedlings 106–107
shade 39, 61
shallots 200–201
sheltering 121
shopping around 30–31
slugs 158–59, 183, 195, 196,
    203, 206, 220, 225
soil 40–49, *see also*
    individual plant types
soil-based compost 42
soil-less compost 45
sowing 102–107
space maximizing 61–63
space saving 18
spearmint 154
spinach 39, 133, 202–203
spraying 153
spring 97
square foot gardening 36, 89
squash 195–96
storage space 52
storing food 132–36
strawberries 143, 219–20
summer 98
sunlight 38–39, 50, 64, 106
supplies 76–77
support systems 51
sustainable planting 51

T
temperature 120
terracotta containers 83–85
thinning out 106, 187
time management 66–70
TimeBanks 67
toilet roll seed trays 180
tomatoes 34, 39, 133, 141,
    143, 176–77

tomato blight 160–61
tomato chutney 147
tomato ketchup 148
tools 32, 51, 77, 243
transplanting 107–112
trolleys for containers 95

U
UV damage to plastic 80

V
vacuum sealers 135
vermiculite 48, 104, 111
vertical gardening 35

W
waste 19, 24, 26
water butts 25
water conservation 25, 39
watering 113–16, 247–48,
    see also individual
    plant types
watering systems 91
weather conditions 21
weeding 31, 119–20,
    167–68
whitefly 177
wicking 248
wind 64
window boxes 34, 62, 90–93
windowsills 34
winter 98
wish-lists 72
wooden containers 93
work sharing 67
wormeries 239
wrought iron containers 91

Z
zucchini *see* courgettes